Table of Contents

Introduction 6

Providing an overview of Book 3 and its focus on the unique journeys of Jennifer Capriati, Mark Philippoussis, and Adriano Panatta. 6

Highlighting the impact of personal and legal challenges, injuries, inconsistency, and limited success outside of clay courts on tennis careers. 11

Introducing Jennifer Capriati, Mark Philippoussis, and Adriano Panatta, setting the stage for their extraordinary stories. 15

Chapter 1: Jennifer Capriati - A Rocky Path to Success 19

Capriati's Early Tennis Years 19

Australian Open Triumph in 2001 23

Personal and Legal Challenges That Interrupted Her Career 27

The Courageous Comeback 31

Chapter 2: Mark Philippoussis - A Promise Unfulfilled 35

Philippoussis's Tennis Beginnings 35

US Open Victory in 1996 39

Injuries That Plagued His Career 43

The Quest for Consistency 47

Chapter 3: Adriano Panatta - King of the Clay Courts 51

Panatta's Tennis Roots 51

French Open Victory in 1976 55

Limited Success Beyond Clay Courts 59

The Challenges of Maintaining Top Form 63

Chapter 4: Battling Life's Curveballs 67

How These Players Faced and Overcame Personal and Professional Challenges 67

Capriati's Inspiring Return to Tennis 71

Philippoussis's Fight Against Injuries 75

Panatta's Struggles Beyond Clay 79

Chapter 5: Life Beyond Tennis 83

Capriati's Life After Competitive Tennis 83

Philippoussis's Career After Hanging Up His Racquet 86

Panatta's Impact and Post-Tennis Pursuits 89

Chapter 6: Legacy and Inspiration 92

The Lasting Impact of These One Slam Wonders 92

Lessons in Resilience and Perseverance 96

Inspiring Others to Overcome Adversity 100

Chapter 7: The Sporting World's Take 133

Insights and Quotes from Tennis Professionals and Experts 133

How These Players Are Remembered in Tennis History . 138

Copyright © 2023 by Ryan P. Parker (Author)

All rights reserved. No part of this book may be reproduced or utilized in any form or by any means, electronic or mechanical, including photocopying, recording or by any information storage and retrieval system, without permission in writing from the publisher, except for brief quotations in critical articles or reviews.

The content of this book is based on various sources and is intended for educational and entertainment purposes only. While the author has made every effort to ensure the accuracy, completeness, and reliability of the information provided, the information may be subject to errors, omissions, or inaccuracies. Therefore, the author makes no warranties, express or implied, regarding the content of this book.

Readers are advised to seek the guidance of a licensed professional before attempting any techniques or actions outlined in this book. The author is not responsible for any losses, damages, or injuries that may arise from the use of information contained within. The information provided in this book is not intended to be a substitute for professional advice, and readers should not rely solely on the information presented.

By reading this book, readers acknowledge that the author is not providing legal, financial, medical, or professional advice. Any reliance on the information contained in this book is solely at the reader's own risk.

Thank you for selecting this book as a valuable source of knowledge and inspiration. Our aim is to provide you with insights and information that will enrich your understanding and enhance your personal growth. We appreciate your decision to embark on this journey of discovery with us, and we hope that this book will exceed your expectations and leave a lasting impact on your life.

Title: Beyond the Baseline: Triumphs and Trials
Subtitle: The Lives of Jennifer Capriati, Mark Philippoussis, and Adriano Panatta

Series: Sports Through Time: A Comprehensive History
Author: Ryan P. Parker

The Cultural and Historical Significance of Their Careers *143*

Conclusion **148**

Reflecting on Remarkable Journeys................................ *148*

The Unique Legacy of Jennifer Capriati, Mark Philippoussis, and Adriano Panatta................................ *153*

Honoring Their Contributions to Tennis History *158*

Wordbook **163**

Supplementary Materials **167**

Introduction

Providing an overview of Book 3 and its focus on the unique journeys of Jennifer Capriati, Mark Philippoussis, and Adriano Panatta.

Tennis, as a sport, is often celebrated for its grand champions, those who hoist multiple Grand Slam trophies high above their heads, etching their names into the annals of history. Yet, amidst the pantheon of tennis legends, there exists a special group – the one-slam wonders, who, despite their remarkable talent and skill, achieved the pinnacle of success just once in their lifetimes. These are the individuals whose stories often remain untold, their struggles overshadowed by the resounding success of their peers. It is the stories of these unsung heroes that we delve into in this book, "Beyond the Baseline: Triumphs and Trials."

In the world of tennis, where champions are celebrated and the spotlight is often reserved for the most triumphant, it is easy to overlook the athletes who navigated a more intricate path—one paved with personal and professional challenges, injuries, inconsistency, and a unique brand of success. It is within the pages of this book that we shine a spotlight on the remarkable journeys of three such players: Jennifer Capriati, Mark Philippoussis, and Adriano Panatta.

Jennifer Capriati - A Rocky Path to Success:

The opening chapter of our journey takes us through the tumultuous career of Jennifer Capriati, a prodigious talent who was thrust into the spotlight at a young age. We will explore Capriati's early years in the tennis world, her extraordinary Australian Open triumph in 2001, and the personal and legal challenges that disrupted her promising career. But perhaps most inspiring of all is her courageous comeback, a testament to the indomitable spirit of a champion.

Mark Philippoussis - A Promise Unfulfilled:

Chapter two unveils the story of Mark Philippoussis, a player who carried the hopes of a nation on his shoulders. We'll journey through his tennis beginnings, reliving his electrifying US Open victory in 1996. Yet, injuries would prove to be his relentless adversary, threatening to overshadow the promise of his talent. As we delve into his quest for consistency, we uncover the determination of a player who never stopped fighting.

Adriano Panatta - King of the Clay Courts:

Our third chapter transports us to the clay courts of Roland Garros, where Adriano Panatta left an indelible mark. We'll trace Panatta's tennis roots, recount his French Open victory in 1976, and ponder the enigma of limited success beyond the clay. In exploring the challenges of maintaining top form, we gain insights into the unique struggles faced by a master of one domain.

Battling Life's Curveballs:

Chapter four is a collective journey, a narrative that weaves the threads of resilience that connect these three exceptional individuals. We delve into how Capriati, Philippoussis, and Panatta faced and overcame personal and professional challenges, their stories interwoven with themes of perseverance and courage. Capriati's inspiring return to tennis, Philippoussis's relentless fight against injuries, and Panatta's ongoing struggles beyond clay serve as powerful testaments to the human spirit's ability to rise above adversity.

Life Beyond Tennis:

Chapter five takes us beyond the tennis court, exploring the lives of these remarkable individuals after they hung up their racquets. What paths did they choose, and how did they navigate the transition from the high-stakes world of professional tennis to the uncharted territory of life after the sport? Their post-tennis pursuits reveal the multi-faceted nature of their characters.

Legacy and Inspiration:

In the penultimate chapter, we examine the lasting impact of these one-slam wonders. Their journeys are not merely stories of personal triumph and tragedy but also sources of inspiration for aspiring athletes and anyone facing adversity. Lessons in resilience and perseverance emerge, reminding us all that victory is not solely measured by the number of trophies on a shelf but by the strength of character forged through trials.

The Sporting World's Take:

The final chapter of our journey is a tapestry woven with insights and quotes from tennis professionals and experts. Here, we gauge how these players are remembered in tennis history and explore the cultural and historical significance of their careers. The echoes of their achievements and challenges resonate not only in the world of tennis but also in the broader context of sports and human perseverance.

In conclusion, "Beyond the Baseline: Triumphs and Trials" is an exploration of the extraordinary journeys of Jennifer Capriati, Mark Philippoussis, and Adriano Panatta, three athletes who, in their own unique ways, left an indelible mark on the world of tennis. Their stories transcend the boundaries of sport, offering lessons in resilience, perseverance, and the enduring human spirit. As we embark on this journey through their triumphs and trials, we honor their contributions to tennis history and celebrate the enduring legacy of the one-slam wonders.

Highlighting the impact of personal and legal challenges, injuries, inconsistency, and limited success outside of clay courts on tennis careers.

Tennis, as a sport, is often celebrated for its grand champions, those who hoist multiple Grand Slam trophies high above their heads, etching their names into the annals of history. Yet, amidst the pantheon of tennis legends, there exists a special group – the one-slam wonders, who, despite their remarkable talent and skill, achieved the pinnacle of success just once in their lifetimes. These are the individuals whose stories often remain untold, their struggles overshadowed by the resounding success of their peers. It is the stories of these unsung heroes that we delve into in this book, "Beyond the Baseline: Triumphs and Trials."

In the world of tennis, where champions are celebrated and the spotlight is often reserved for the most triumphant, it is easy to overlook the athletes who navigated a more intricate path—one paved with personal and professional challenges, injuries, inconsistency, and a unique brand of success. It is within the pages of this book that we shine a spotlight on the remarkable journeys of three such players: Jennifer Capriati, Mark Philippoussis, and Adriano Panatta.

The Impact of Personal and Legal Challenges:

The tennis world is no stranger to the weight of personal and legal challenges that can bear down upon even the most promising careers. For Jennifer Capriati, her meteoric rise to fame was juxtaposed with a series of personal and legal challenges that threatened to derail her career before it truly began. These challenges left a profound impact, altering the course of her journey and shaping her into the resilient figure she would later become. We will explore the intricacies of her struggles and the strength it took to overcome them.

Injuries: The Silent Adversaries:

In the realm of professional sports, injuries are a ubiquitous and often cruel companion. For Mark Philippoussis, a player with immense promise and raw power, injuries became the silent adversaries that lurked in the shadows of his career. His quest for consistency was repeatedly interrupted by physical setbacks, each recovery serving as a testament to his unwavering determination. We will delve into the physical and emotional toll that injuries exacted on his journey and the unwavering spirit that carried him through the darkest times.

The Battle with Inconsistency:

Inconsistency is the nemesis of every athlete, a shadow that looms over even the brightest talents. Adriano

Panatta, the "King of the Clay Courts," faced a unique brand of inconsistency—one that took hold beyond the familiar confines of clay. His struggles to replicate his clay court successes on other surfaces presented a challenge that few players have encountered. We will explore the psychological and strategic battles Panatta waged as he sought to transcend the label that confined him.

Limited Success Outside of Clay Courts:

The tennis world is marked by its diversity of playing surfaces, each demanding a distinct set of skills and adaptability. For Panatta, the allure of clay was undeniable, and his victories at the French Open were iconic. Yet, his success on clay was juxtaposed with limited triumphs on other surfaces, sparking debates about his versatility as a player. We will unravel the intricacies of Panatta's game and the hurdles he faced as he ventured beyond the comfort of the clay courts.

As we embark on this journey through the lives of Jennifer Capriati, Mark Philippoussis, and Adriano Panatta, we will delve deep into the profound impact of personal and legal challenges, injuries, inconsistency, and the quest for success beyond the clay courts. Their stories are not just narratives of tennis careers but reflections of the human spirit's ability to overcome the most formidable obstacles.

"Beyond the Baseline: Triumphs and Trials" is a tribute to their resilience and an exploration of the indomitable will that defined their journeys.

Introducing Jennifer Capriati, Mark Philippoussis, and Adriano Panatta, setting the stage for their extraordinary stories.

Tennis, as a sport, is often celebrated for its grand champions, those who hoist multiple Grand Slam trophies high above their heads, etching their names into the annals of history. Yet, amidst the pantheon of tennis legends, there exists a special group – the one-slam wonders, who, despite their remarkable talent and skill, achieved the pinnacle of success just once in their lifetimes. These are the individuals whose stories often remain untold, their struggles overshadowed by the resounding success of their peers. It is the stories of these unsung heroes that we delve into in this book, "Beyond the Baseline: Triumphs and Trials."

In the world of tennis, where champions are celebrated and the spotlight is often reserved for the most triumphant, it is easy to overlook the athletes who navigated a more intricate path—one paved with personal and professional challenges, injuries, inconsistency, and a unique brand of success. It is within the pages of this book that we shine a spotlight on the remarkable journeys of three such players: Jennifer Capriati, Mark Philippoussis, and Adriano Panatta.

Introducing Jennifer Capriati:

Jennifer Capriati, a name that resonates through the annals of tennis history as a symbol of promise, tumult, and redemption. Her story begins as a young prodigy, hailed as the next big thing in women's tennis. From a tender age, she exhibited a raw talent and fearless aggression that promised to reshape the women's game. We will journey through her early years in the tennis world, where the weight of expectation rested heavily on her shoulders.

Capriati's extraordinary rise to stardom was punctuated by her Australian Open triumph in 2001, a moment that sent shockwaves through the tennis world. However, as swiftly as she ascended, her career was marred by personal and legal challenges that threatened to eclipse her potential. We will delve into the complexities of her struggles and the courage it took to face them head-on.

Introducing Mark Philippoussis:

Mark Philippoussis, a towering figure on the tennis court, was heralded as the great hope of Australian tennis. With a powerful serve that could overpower the most formidable opponents, Philippoussis burst onto the scene in the 1990s, capturing hearts and imaginations alike. We will uncover the beginnings of his tennis journey, tracing the path that led him to a memorable US Open victory in 1996, a triumph that sparked national pride.

Yet, Philippoussis's journey was marked by a relentless adversary—injuries. These silent adversaries, lurking in the background, would go on to test his resolve and shape his character. We will explore the physical and emotional toll of injuries on his career and the unwavering spirit that carried him through the darkest times.

Introducing Adriano Panatta:

Adriano Panatta, the enigmatic "King of the Clay Courts," casts a unique shadow across the world of tennis. His journey began amidst the beauty and artistry of Italian tennis, and his rise to prominence on the clay courts of Roland Garros is the stuff of legends. We will trace his tennis roots and relive his French Open victory in 1976, a victory that solidified his status as a clay court maestro.

Yet, Panatta's career was marked by a curious duality—an unparalleled dominance on clay juxtaposed with limited success on other surfaces. The challenges of replicating his clay court magic on foreign terrains became a puzzle that would define his career. We will explore the intricacies of his game and the hurdles he faced as he ventured beyond the comfort of clay.

As we embark on this journey through the lives of Jennifer Capriati, Mark Philippoussis, and Adriano Panatta, we are confronted with the rich tapestry of human stories that tennis weaves. Their lives and careers transcend the confines of a tennis court, offering insights into the indomitable human spirit and its capacity for triumph in the face of adversity. "Beyond the Baseline: Triumphs and Trials" is a tribute to their resilience and an exploration of the unique legacies they leave behind.

Chapter 1: Jennifer Capriati - A Rocky Path to Success

Capriati's Early Tennis Years

Before the world knew her as a Grand Slam champion, Jennifer Maria Capriati was a name whispered with reverence in the corridors of junior tennis. Born on March 29, 1976, in New York, Jennifer was destined to be a tennis prodigy. The Capriati family, deeply involved in tennis, provided the nurturing soil from which this young talent would grow into a force to be reckoned with on the tennis court.

A Tennis Family:

In the Capriati household, tennis was not just a sport; it was a way of life. Jennifer's father, Stefano Capriati, was an accomplished tennis coach, and her mother, Denise Capriati, nurtured her talent from an early age. The tennis racquet was almost an extension of Jennifer's hand, and it was evident that she possessed a natural gift for the sport.

Jennifer's early years were marked by countless hours spent on the court, hitting balls with a fervor that belied her tender age. She was a pint-sized powerhouse, showing remarkable speed, agility, and an innate understanding of the game. Her prodigious talent quickly caught the attention of coaches and competitors alike, setting the stage for her meteoric rise.

The Junior Sensation:

Jennifer's prowess on the junior circuit was nothing short of extraordinary. Her name became synonymous with victory as she blazed through the ranks, dominating opponents with a combination of power and finesse that was beyond her years. At the age of 13, she became the youngest player to win the French Open junior title, a milestone that hinted at the greatness to come.

Her victory in the junior division of the 1989 US Open further solidified her reputation as a rising star. She possessed an uncanny ability to read her opponents, adapting her game effortlessly to exploit weaknesses. The tennis world watched in awe as Jennifer Capriati, barely a teenager, navigated the world of professional tennis with the poise of a seasoned veteran.

The Transition to the Pros:

As Jennifer's junior career reached its zenith, the inevitable question arose: Would she be able to transition her prodigious talent to the professional tour? The pressure was immense, and the expectations were sky-high. The tennis world eagerly awaited her debut, hoping to witness the emergence of a new tennis sensation.

In March 1990, at the age of 13, Jennifer Capriati took her first steps into the world of professional tennis. Her debut was met with a blend of excitement and skepticism. Could a player so young truly compete at the highest level of the sport? The doubts were soon dispelled as Jennifer displayed a level of maturity and composure that belied her age.

Her early matches on the professional circuit were marked by flashes of brilliance interspersed with moments of youthful exuberance. But with each outing, she gained valuable experience, learning to harness her power and refine her game. It was clear that Jennifer Capriati was a force to be reckoned with, and her journey had only just begun.

The Path Forward:

As we delve into the early tennis years of Jennifer Capriati, we witness the birth of a tennis prodigy, a young player whose talent defied her age. Her formative years on the tennis court laid the foundation for a career that would be marked by both triumph and adversity. In the pages that follow, we will explore the highs and lows of Capriati's journey, from her remarkable victories to the personal and legal challenges that would disrupt her promising career. But before we venture into those tumultuous chapters, we must first understand the extraordinary promise and potential that defined Jennifer Capriati's early years in tennis.

Australian Open Triumph in 2001

In the annals of tennis history, there are moments that transcend the boundaries of the sport, moments that capture the essence of human resilience and the unwavering spirit of a champion. Jennifer Capriati's triumphant victory at the Australian Open in 2001 is one such moment—a watershed in her career and a testament to her indomitable will.

A Return to Prominence:

Jennifer Capriati's early years in professional tennis were marked by the promise of greatness, but they were also marred by the weight of immense expectations and the trappings of fame. The prodigious talent that had propelled her to the top of the junior circuit faced the harsh realities of the professional tour. Injuries, inconsistency, and personal struggles cast a shadow over her career, causing many to doubt whether she would ever fulfill her potential.

As the years passed, Capriati's presence on the tennis circuit became increasingly sporadic. Her ranking plummeted, and she seemed destined to become one of the sport's "what could have been" stories. It was during this period of uncertainty and introspection that she made a decision that would alter the course of her career.

The Road to Redemption:

Jennifer Capriati's journey to redemption was not a straightforward one. It was a path filled with setbacks and doubts, a path that required her to confront her personal demons and rebuild her game from the ground up. But at the core of her journey was a fierce determination to prove to herself and the world that she could overcome the odds and rise to the pinnacle of tennis once again.

Her return to professional tennis in the late 1990s was met with both curiosity and skepticism. Could a player who had been away from the game for so long rediscover her form and competitiveness? The doubts only fueled Capriati's resolve. She embarked on a grueling journey of physical and mental conditioning, working tirelessly to regain her fitness and fine-tune her skills.

The Cinderella Run:

The year 2001 dawned with Jennifer Capriati ranked far from the upper echelons of women's tennis. However, it was the Australian Open that would provide the backdrop for one of the most remarkable Cinderella stories in the sport's history. As the tournament unfolded, Capriati began her ascent through the draw, dispatching higher-ranked opponents with a mix of power and finesse that harked back to her prodigious junior days.

Her path to the final was punctuated by thrilling encounters, each victory a testament to her unwavering resolve. The semifinal clash against Martina Hingis, the world No. 1 at the time, was a defining moment. Capriati's steely determination and never-say-die attitude saw her through a grueling three-set battle, earning her a place in the championship match.

The Final Triumph:

On January 27, 2001, Jennifer Capriati stood on the cusp of history. She faced off against Kim Clijsters in the final, a match that would not only determine the Australian Open champion but also solidify Capriati's remarkable comeback. The tension in the air was palpable as the two players battled for supremacy on the Melbourne Park courts.

In a hard-fought contest that spanned three sets, Capriati displayed the heart and grit of a true champion. Her powerful groundstrokes and relentless determination saw her emerge victorious, clinching her first Grand Slam title in over a decade. As she lifted the championship trophy high above her head, tears of joy and redemption flowed freely—a poignant moment that resonated with tennis fans worldwide.

Legacy of Resilience:

Jennifer Capriati's Australian Open triumph in 2001 is more than a tennis victory; it is a story of redemption and resilience. It serves as a testament to the human spirit's capacity to overcome adversity and reclaim lost glory. Her journey from prodigious talent to fallen star to triumphant champion is a narrative that continues to inspire athletes and fans alike, reminding us all that the path to success is rarely linear, but with unwavering determination, it is always attainable. In the chapters that follow, we will explore the highs and lows that followed this momentous victory and the enduring legacy it left on the world of tennis.

Personal and Legal Challenges That Interrupted Her Career

Jennifer Capriati's journey to tennis stardom was not just about powerful serves and precise groundstrokes; it was also marked by a series of personal and legal challenges that tested her resilience and threatened to derail her promising career. In this chapter, we delve into the tumultuous period in Capriati's life when off-court struggles cast a shadow over her tennis aspirations.

The Burden of Expectations:

From a young age, Jennifer Capriati was hailed as the future of women's tennis. The weight of expectation was immense, and it proved to be a double-edged sword. While her prodigious talent propelled her to the top ranks of the sport, it also exposed her to unprecedented levels of scrutiny and pressure. Capriati became a global sensation, a teen sensation, and the tennis world watched her every move with anticipation.

The relentless spotlight took its toll on Capriati's psyche. She was not just a tennis player; she was a symbol of promise, and the expectations were often suffocating. The transition from a carefree child prodigy to a professional athlete burdened with the hopes of an entire sport was a challenging one, and it set the stage for the personal challenges that would follow.

The Dark Period:

Amidst the glare of the tennis spotlight, Jennifer Capriati began to grapple with personal demons. The pressures of fame and the weight of expectations led her down a path of rebellion and self-destruction. Her struggles with substance abuse became public knowledge, casting a pall over her career and personal life.

During this dark period, Capriati's tennis career was on hold. She struggled with her inner demons and navigated the complexities of addiction. It was a tumultuous time for the young athlete, a time when her tennis talents lay dormant, overshadowed by the battles she waged off the court.

Legal Troubles:

As Jennifer Capriati grappled with personal demons, legal troubles also surfaced, further complicating her life. In 1993, she faced legal consequences related to shoplifting, an incident that garnered widespread media attention. The incident marked a low point in her life and fueled concerns about her well-being.

The legal challenges added another layer of complexity to Capriati's tumultuous journey. They not only had implications for her personal life but also disrupted her tennis career. The legal battles cast a long shadow over her prospects on the professional circuit, leaving her future in the sport uncertain.

The Road to Redemption:

Amidst the personal and legal challenges that seemed insurmountable, Jennifer Capriati embarked on a journey of redemption. The path to recovery was arduous, filled with setbacks and moments of doubt. But at its core was Capriati's unyielding determination to regain control of her life and resurrect her tennis career.

The road to redemption was not without its share of skeptics and naysayers. Many doubted whether Capriati could overcome her troubled past and return to the tennis court with the same vigor and passion that had defined her early years. However, she was determined to prove them wrong.

The Comeback:

Jennifer Capriati's return to professional tennis was nothing short of remarkable. Her comeback was marked by an unwavering commitment to fitness, training, and mental strength. She shed the demons of her past and embraced a new chapter in her life and career.

As we explore the personal and legal challenges that interrupted Jennifer Capriati's career, we also bear witness to her indomitable spirit and resilience. Her journey serves as a powerful reminder that athletes, like all individuals, face trials and tribulations. What defines them is not the adversity they encounter, but their ability to rise above it. In the chapters that follow, we will delve deeper into Capriati's courageous comeback and the triumphs and trials that would shape her career.

The Courageous Comeback

The tale of Jennifer Capriati is one of remarkable twists and turns, a rollercoaster ride through the heights of promise and the depths of personal and legal challenges. But it is also a story of redemption and resilience—a story of a courageous comeback that would see her rise from the ashes of her past and reclaim her place in the world of professional tennis.

The Turning Point:

For Jennifer Capriati, the turning point came when she confronted the demons that had haunted her for years. The battles with substance abuse, the legal troubles, and the personal turmoil had left her at a crossroads. It was a pivotal moment in her life, one where she had to decide whether to succumb to the weight of her past or summon the strength to carve a new path.

Capriati chose the latter. She made the brave decision to confront her issues head-on, seeking the help and support she needed to overcome her personal challenges. It was a journey fraught with difficulty and self-discovery, but it was also a journey that would ultimately pave the way for her comeback.

The Grueling Path to Fitness:

One of the most remarkable aspects of Jennifer Capriati's comeback was her unwavering commitment to physical fitness. She embarked on an intensive regimen that would not only bring her back to peak playing condition but also transform her into one of the fittest athletes on the women's tour.

The road to fitness was grueling, marked by rigorous training sessions, strict dietary discipline, and an unwavering focus on her physical well-being. Capriati's determination was evident as she shed excess weight, increased her strength and endurance, and emerged as a formidable force on the tennis court once again.

Mental Resilience and Emotional Healing:

The comeback was not just about physical transformation; it was also about mental resilience and emotional healing. Capriati worked closely with sports psychologists to strengthen her mental fortitude, enabling her to cope with the pressures of professional tennis and the weight of her past.

She faced the judgment and skepticism of the tennis world, which questioned whether she could regain her form and competitiveness. Yet, Capriati's mental resilience allowed her to block out the noise and focus on her game.

She embraced a positive mindset, a sense of purpose, and a newfound appreciation for the opportunities that lay ahead.

The Return to Competition:

Jennifer Capriati's return to professional tennis was met with curiosity, anticipation, and trepidation. It marked a triumphant comeback to a sport that had once been her playground and her crucible. Her first matches back on the tour were met with mixed results, but they showcased glimpses of her undeniable talent and fighting spirit.

As she regained her match fitness and reacquainted herself with the demands of professional tennis, Capriati's game continued to evolve. Her powerful baseline game and aggressive style remained intact, but she added new dimensions to her play, incorporating improved tactics and shot selection.

The Australian Open Triumph Revisited:

Jennifer Capriati's comeback reached its zenith at the Australian Open in 2001. The same tournament that had witnessed her struggles a decade earlier would now become the stage for her triumphant return. Her victory in Melbourne was not just a testament to her tennis skills but also a testament to her unbreakable spirit.

The Australian Open triumph of 2001 was a reaffirmation of Capriati's place among the tennis elite. It was a victory that transcended the sport, a symbol of redemption and resilience. As she lifted the championship trophy, it was a moment not only of personal triumph but also of inspiration for all who had followed her journey.

Legacy of Courage:

Jennifer Capriati's courageous comeback remains one of the most inspiring chapters in the annals of tennis history. It serves as a reminder that setbacks are not the end of the road but opportunities for growth and transformation. Her story is a testament to the power of determination, resilience, and the human spirit's capacity for redemption.

In the chapters that follow, we will explore the highs and lows that Jennifer Capriati encountered on her journey, as well as the enduring legacy she left on the world of tennis. Her comeback is a story of triumph over adversity—a story that continues to inspire athletes and individuals alike to persevere in the face of life's challenges.

Chapter 2: Mark Philippoussis - A Promise Unfulfilled

Philippoussis's Tennis Beginnings

Mark Philippoussis, often affectionately referred to as the "Scud" for his thunderous serves, was destined for a tennis journey that would capture the imagination of the sport's enthusiasts worldwide. In this chapter, we explore the early years of a young Australian with a gift for tennis, whose talent would propel him onto the global stage.

A Tennis Family's Legacy:

Mark Philippoussis was born on November 7, 1976, in Melbourne, Australia. From an early age, he was immersed in the world of tennis. His father, Nick Philippoussis, was a tennis coach and played a pivotal role in shaping his son's future. Under his guidance, Mark's tennis education began almost as soon as he could hold a racket.

The Philippoussis family's dedication to tennis was not confined to the coaching expertise of Mark's father alone. His mother, Rossana, was a former professional player, and his sister, Patina, also embarked on a tennis career. Tennis was more than a sport for the Philippoussis family; it was a way of life.

The Junior Prodigy:

Mark Philippoussis's journey as a tennis prodigy began to take shape during his early years. His natural athleticism and hand-eye coordination made him a standout on the junior circuit in Australia. His powerful serve, which would later become his trademark, was already in evidence, sending ripples of excitement through the tennis community.

As a junior player, Philippoussis garnered attention not only for his skill but also for his fierce competitiveness on the court. He possessed an innate ability to stay cool under pressure, a trait that would serve him well in his future battles on the professional tour.

Coaching and Mentorship:

Mark Philippoussis's talent and potential were too evident to go unnoticed. He began receiving coaching and mentorship from some of the most respected figures in Australian tennis. In particular, Tony Roche, a renowned coach who had worked with tennis legends like Ivan Lendl and Pat Rafter, played a pivotal role in refining Philippoussis's game.

Under Roche's guidance, Philippoussis honed his skills, developing a powerful and versatile game that would later make him a force to be reckoned with on both grass and hard courts. The coaching and mentorship he received during his formative years provided him with the tools he needed to compete at the highest levels of professional tennis.

The Transition to the Pros:

Mark Philippoussis made his debut on the professional tour in the early 1990s. His transition to the pros was marked by a seamless blend of raw talent and the skills he had refined under the guidance of coaches like Tony Roche. As he faced off against seasoned professionals, he displayed a fearless brand of tennis that captivated audiences.

One of the early highlights of his career came in 1996 when he reached the final of the U.S. Open. While he ultimately fell short in the championship match, his performance announced his arrival as a formidable contender on the Grand Slam stage. It was a glimpse of the promise that lay ahead, a promise that would be accompanied by its own set of challenges and triumphs.

The Road to Promise:

As we delve into the beginnings of Mark Philippoussis's tennis journey, we encounter the foundations of a career that promised greatness. His upbringing in a tennis family, his early experiences as a junior prodigy, and the coaching and mentorship he received all played pivotal roles in shaping the tennis phenomenon known as the "Scud."

In the chapters that follow, we will explore the highs and lows, the triumphs and trials that marked Philippoussis's path in professional tennis. His journey is a testament to the enduring appeal of tennis as a sport and the extraordinary potential that can be nurtured from a young age.

US Open Victory in 1996

In the world of tennis, Grand Slam victories are the pinnacle of achievement—a testament to a player's skill, determination, and mental fortitude. For Mark Philippoussis, a young Australian with a blistering serve and a charismatic presence, the US Open victory in 1996 would mark a defining moment in his career and a glimpse into the promise that had always surrounded him.

The Path to the US Open:

Mark Philippoussis arrived at the 1996 US Open with a sense of purpose and ambition. At just 19 years old, he had already made waves on the professional tour, showcasing his powerful game and unbridled enthusiasm. His journey to the US Open title would be marked by a series of enthralling matches that showcased his formidable potential.

As the tournament progressed, Philippoussis's powerful serves and explosive groundstrokes drew the attention of fans and experts alike. His aggressive style of play, combined with a fearlessness that belied his age, made him a formidable opponent on the fast hard courts of Flushing Meadows.

The Semifinal Showdown:

One of the defining moments of the 1996 US Open was Mark Philippoussis's semifinal clash against Pete

Sampras, the reigning world No. 1 and a tennis icon. Sampras, known for his dominance on hard courts, was the overwhelming favorite. However, Philippoussis, undaunted by the occasion, stepped onto the court with a belief in his abilities.

The semifinal match between Philippoussis and Sampras was an epic battle that captivated tennis fans around the world. Philippoussis's thunderous serves and fearless shot-making pushed Sampras to his limits. In a thrilling five-set encounter, Philippoussis emerged victorious, defeating the world No. 1 and earning his place in the championship match.

The Championship Moment:

On September 8, 1996, Mark Philippoussis stood on the brink of tennis history. He faced off against another rising star, the Dutch player Richard Krajicek, in the US Open final. The match was a clash of titans, with both players known for their powerful serves and aggressive playing styles.

In a performance that showcased his remarkable talent and composure, Philippoussis defeated Krajicek in straight sets, capturing his first Grand Slam title. As he raised the championship trophy above his head, it was a moment of triumph and promise fulfilled—a promise that had been evident since his early years as a junior prodigy.

The Impact of Victory:

Mark Philippoussis's US Open victory in 1996 had a profound impact on the tennis world. It announced the arrival of a new generation of players, marked by their athleticism and aggressive playing styles. Philippoussis, with his charisma and powerful game, became a fan favorite and a symbol of the sport's evolution.

The victory also elevated Philippoussis to the upper echelons of men's tennis. He was hailed as a future Grand Slam champion, and the tennis community eagerly awaited his future successes. His triumph in New York was not just a personal milestone but a moment of promise for Australian tennis and a beacon for aspiring young players around the world.

The Legacy of 1996:

As we revisit Mark Philippoussis's US Open victory in 1996, we are reminded of the electrifying potential that had always surrounded him. It was a moment of promise fulfilled, a glimpse into the future of men's tennis. However, it was also a moment that would come to define the narrative of Philippoussis's career—an immense promise that, for various reasons, would remain largely unfulfilled.

In the chapters that follow, we will explore the challenges and setbacks that would test Philippoussis's resilience and shape the trajectory of his career. His US Open victory in 1996 serves as a poignant reminder of the fleeting nature of success in professional tennis and the enduring allure of the Grand Slam stage.

Injuries That Plagued His Career

In the tumultuous world of professional tennis, the road to success is often riddled with physical challenges that test an athlete's mettle. For Mark Philippoussis, a player known for his explosive power and charisma, injuries would become a recurring theme in his career, threatening to derail the promise he had shown as a young champion.

The Physical Toll of the Game:

Professional tennis demands a physical toll that few sports can match. The relentless grind of training, the demands of a packed tournament schedule, and the high-impact nature of the sport itself place immense strain on an athlete's body. Mark Philippoussis, with his dynamic playing style centered around a booming serve and aggressive baseline game, was no exception.

As Philippoussis ascended the ranks of professional tennis, his body bore the brunt of the physical demands. The explosive power that defined his game also made him susceptible to injuries. His serve, one of the fastest in the history of the sport, placed tremendous strain on his shoulder, and his relentless movement on the court took its toll on his knees.

The Shoulder Injury:

One of the most persistent and debilitating injuries that plagued Mark Philippoussis was his shoulder injury. The repeated stress placed on his shoulder joint, particularly during the serve, led to a series of setbacks that would haunt him throughout his career.

The shoulder injury first surfaced in the late 1990s, shortly after his breakthrough victory at the US Open in 1996. It forced him to withdraw from tournaments and undergo extensive rehabilitation. Despite his efforts to recover, the injury would resurface repeatedly, casting a shadow over his career.

Knee Troubles:

In addition to the shoulder injury, Mark Philippoussis battled persistent knee problems. The rigorous movement and explosive changes in direction that characterized his game took a toll on his knees, leading to chronic issues that hampered his mobility and overall performance.

The knee troubles forced Philippoussis to make adjustments to his playing style. He had to manage his movement more carefully on the court, and at times, he struggled to chase down balls and cover the court as effectively as he had in his earlier years.

The Cycle of Recovery and Setback:

Throughout his career, Mark Philippoussis found himself caught in a cycle of recovery and setback. Each time he battled through an injury, he would make a valiant comeback, showcasing the same explosive power and talent that had earned him acclaim. However, the physical toll of the sport would often rear its head again, leading to frustrating periods of inactivity and rehabilitation.

The cycle of injury and recovery took an emotional toll on Philippoussis as well. He faced the challenge of maintaining his mental fortitude and self-belief in the face of recurrent setbacks. It was a test of his resilience as both a player and an individual.

The Impact on Career Trajectory:

The injuries that plagued Mark Philippoussis undoubtedly had a profound impact on the trajectory of his career. They prevented him from achieving the level of consistency and success that had been expected of him after his early triumphs. Grand Slam titles, which had once seemed within reach, remained elusive.

The injuries forced Philippoussis to withdraw from tournaments, miss opportunities, and endure the frustration of interrupted momentum. They also necessitated adjustments to his playing style and training regimen, which at times affected his overall competitiveness.

Legacy of Promise and Perseverance:

Mark Philippoussis's career is a testament to the challenges that professional athletes face, particularly in a physically demanding sport like tennis. While injuries may have derailed some of his aspirations, they did not diminish the promise and charisma that made him a beloved figure in the tennis world.

In the chapters that follow, we will delve deeper into the trials and tribulations that shaped Philippoussis's career. His story is one of promise unfulfilled, but it is also a story of perseverance and the enduring allure of a sport that tests the limits of the human body and spirit.

The Quest for Consistency

Consistency is the bedrock of success in professional tennis. While Mark Philippoussis possessed the raw power and charisma to compete with the best, his career was marked by a perpetual quest for consistency—a quest that would define his journey in the sport.

The Peaks and Valleys:

Mark Philippoussis's career was punctuated by dazzling peaks and frustrating valleys. At his best, he could defeat the world's top players with ease, showcasing a game that combined a thunderous serve with blistering groundstrokes. However, his inconsistency would often leave fans and pundits scratching their heads.

One of the challenges Philippoussis faced was the unpredictability of his game. He could produce stunning performances on one day and falter unexpectedly in the next match. The inconsistency extended to his results in Grand Slam tournaments, where his path to success was often characterized by erratic performances.

The Mental Component:

In the quest for consistency, the mental aspect of the game played a pivotal role. Philippoussis possessed the physical tools to compete at the highest level, but he also needed the mental fortitude to navigate the pressures and uncertainties of professional tennis.

Throughout his career, Philippoussis worked with sports psychologists and mental coaches to strengthen his mental resilience. He sought to harness his focus and concentration, particularly during critical moments in matches. The mental component of consistency was a constant area of focus and growth for him.

Injury-Related Setbacks:

As discussed earlier, injuries were a significant factor that plagued Mark Philippoussis's career. Each injury setback not only disrupted his physical preparation but also affected his rhythm and confidence on the court. It was a vicious cycle where injuries led to inconsistency, and inconsistency sometimes contributed to further injuries.

Managing injuries and their impact on his game became a recurring challenge for Philippoussis. The delicate balance between pushing his body to perform at its best and avoiding overexertion to prevent injury was a constant juggling act.

Adjustments to Playing Style:

In his pursuit of consistency, Philippoussis also made adjustments to his playing style. He recognized that his aggressive, high-risk style of play sometimes led to unnecessary errors and fluctuations in performance. To address this, he worked on improving his shot selection and minimizing unforced errors.

The adjustments also extended to his approach in matches. Philippoussis became more tactically aware, focusing on constructing points and rallies rather than relying solely on his power. These strategic changes aimed to enhance his ability to maintain a consistent level of play.

The Elusive Grand Slam Glory:

Mark Philippoussis's quest for consistency was most evident in his pursuit of Grand Slam glory. While he reached the pinnacle of success with his US Open victory in 1996, he struggled to replicate that success on the sport's biggest stages. Inconsistent performances at Grand Slam tournaments, often punctuated by early exits, left him with a sense of unfulfilled promise.

The Grand Slam tournaments, where Philippoussis's talent was most keenly scrutinized, became both a source of inspiration and frustration. He knew he had the ability to compete for major titles, but his inconsistency prevented him from achieving the sustained success he desired.

Legacy of the Journey:

Mark Philippoussis's quest for consistency is a recurring theme in his career—a quest marked by its challenges and triumphs. While he may not have achieved the level of consistency that some of his contemporaries did, his journey serves as a reminder of the complexities and demands of professional tennis.

In the chapters that follow, we will explore the highs and lows, the victories and defeats, and the enduring allure of a sport that continually tests the limits of an athlete's physical and mental capabilities. Philippoussis's career is a testament to the pursuit of greatness, even in the face of inconsistency, and the enduring allure of the tennis court.

Chapter 3: Adriano Panatta - King of the Clay Courts

Panatta's Tennis Roots

Before Adriano Panatta became known as the "King of the Clay Courts," his journey in the world of tennis began in the vibrant landscape of Italian tennis, where passion for the sport and dedication ran deep. In this chapter, we delve into Panatta's tennis roots and the early influences that shaped his extraordinary career.

The Italian Tennis Scene:

Adriano Panatta was born on July 9, 1950, in Rome, Italy—a city known for its rich cultural history and deep appreciation for sports, including tennis. Italy had a burgeoning tennis scene, with a growing number of young talents aspiring to make their mark on the international stage.

From a young age, Panatta was immersed in this tennis culture. His family, particularly his father, recognized his early aptitude for the sport and nurtured his passion. Tennis was more than just a recreational activity; it was a way of life that would define Panatta's future.

Early Years on the Court:

Panatta's journey on the tennis court began with modest beginnings. He started playing tennis at a local club in Rome, honing his skills on the clay courts that would become synonymous with his name. His early experiences on the court instilled in him a deep love for the game and a hunger for improvement.

As a junior player, Panatta displayed natural talent and a fierce competitive spirit. He quickly rose through the ranks of Italian junior tennis, earning recognition for his skills and determination. It was evident that he possessed the raw ingredients of a future tennis star.

Mentorship and Coaching:

The guidance and mentorship Panatta received during his formative years were instrumental in shaping his tennis journey. Coaches and mentors recognized his potential and provided valuable insights into the technical and strategic aspects of the game.

One of the pivotal figures in Panatta's early development was his coach and mentor, Francesco De Benedittis. De Benedittis not only refined Panatta's technique but also instilled in him the discipline and work ethic required to succeed at the highest level of professional tennis.

The Rise of an Italian Star:

Adriano Panatta's rise as a tennis star was marked by a series of milestones in the Italian tennis landscape. He made his mark in national competitions and quickly transitioned to the international stage. His performances on the European circuit garnered attention, and he began to establish himself as one of Italy's top tennis talents.

One of the highlights of Panatta's early career was his victory in the Italian Open in 1973. This win on the iconic clay courts of Rome marked a turning point in his career and solidified his reputation as a formidable clay-court specialist. It was a moment of pride for Italian tennis and a prelude to his future success.

The Clay-Court Expertise:

The clay courts of Europe, with their distinctive characteristics and slower surface, would become the canvas on which Adriano Panatta painted his tennis masterpiece. His expertise on clay was honed through years of dedication and countless hours of practice on this unique surface.

Panatta's mastery of clay-court tennis was characterized by his exceptional movement, precise shot-making, and an uncanny ability to slide on the surface. These skills, combined with his competitive fire, made him a formidable opponent on clay and earned him the moniker "King of the Clay Courts."

Legacy of Italian Tennis:

As we explore Adriano Panatta's tennis roots, we gain insights into the foundations of a career that would leave an indelible mark on Italian tennis. His journey from the clay courts of Rome to the international tennis circuit serves as a testament to the passion and dedication that define the sport.

In the chapters that follow, we will delve deeper into Panatta's remarkable victories and challenges, his enduring impact on the sport of tennis, and his status as one of Italy's most iconic tennis figures. His tennis roots in Italy would provide the fertile soil from which his extraordinary career would spring forth, ultimately leaving an enduring legacy in the world of tennis.

French Open Victory in 1976

Adriano Panatta's legacy as the "King of the Clay Courts" was solidified on the hallowed grounds of Roland Garros in 1976. His remarkable victory at the French Open that year not only made him a tennis icon but also etched his name in the annals of sports history. In this section, we relive the unforgettable moments of Panatta's triumph on the red clay of Paris.

The Clay-Court Maestro:

By the mid-1970s, Adriano Panatta had established himself as a dominant force on the clay courts of Europe. His mastery of the surface, characterized by exquisite shot-making and unparalleled movement, made him a formidable opponent on clay. However, the French Open remained an unconquered summit in his career.

As the 1976 French Open approached, Panatta's reputation as a clay-court maestro loomed large. The anticipation and expectations surrounding his performance were palpable, and he carried the hopes of Italian tennis on his shoulders.

The Path to Glory:

Panatta's journey to the 1976 French Open title was a testament to his skill, resilience, and unwavering determination. The road to glory was marked by grueling battles on the clay courts of Roland Garros, where he faced formidable opponents in every round.

One of the defining moments of his campaign came in the quarterfinals when he clashed with the legendary Bjorn Borg. Borg, a dominant force on clay himself, was considered nearly unbeatable on the surface. Yet, in a thrilling encounter, Panatta emerged victorious, defeating the tennis prodigy and signaling his intent to capture the title.

The Championship Match:

In the final of the 1976 French Open, Adriano Panatta faced Harold Solomon, an American player known for his consistency and defensive prowess. The matchup promised an intriguing clash of styles, with Panatta's aggressive shot-making pitted against Solomon's defensive skills.

The final match was a closely contested affair, with both players showcasing their tennis prowess. Panatta's powerful forehand and deft touch at the net were on full display, while Solomon's defensive prowess tested Panatta's patience and shot selection.

After a grueling five-set battle that captivated tennis fans around the world, Panatta emerged as the victor, winning his first and only French Open title. The moment was one of sheer jubilation as he raised the championship trophy, draped in the Italian flag, on the red clay of Roland Garros.

The Impact of Victory:

Adriano Panatta's French Open victory in 1976 was not just a personal triumph but a historic moment for Italian tennis. He became the first Italian player to win a Grand Slam singles title since Nicola Pietrangeli's victory at the same tournament in 1960.

The impact of Panatta's victory reverberated across Italy and the tennis world. It ignited a surge of interest in tennis in Italy, inspiring a new generation of players and fans. Panatta's charismatic style of play and his ability to capture the hearts of spectators further cemented his status as a national hero.

The Enduring Legacy:

As we revisit Adriano Panatta's French Open victory in 1976, we are reminded of the remarkable achievements that defined his career. It was a moment of tennis history that showcased his clay-court mastery and indomitable spirit. Panatta's triumph in Paris remains a source of pride for Italian tennis and a testament to the enduring allure of the clay courts.

In the chapters that follow, we will explore the highs and lows of Panatta's career, his continued impact on the sport, and his status as a legendary figure in the world of tennis. The French Open victory of 1976 was not just a crowning achievement but a timeless reminder of the enduring legacy of the "King of the Clay Courts."

Limited Success Beyond Clay Courts

While Adriano Panatta's dominance on clay courts was unquestionable, his success on other surfaces, particularly grass and hard courts, remained somewhat elusive. In this section, we explore Panatta's challenges and limited success when transitioning away from his beloved clay courts.

The Clay-Court Specialist:

Adriano Panatta's affinity for clay courts was rooted in his exceptional skill set and playing style. His ability to slide on the surface, impeccable topspin forehand, and net-rushing tactics made him a formidable force on clay. However, the transition to other surfaces posed distinct challenges for the "King of the Clay Courts."

The Grass-Court Dilemma:

Grass courts, with their low bounce and faster pace, presented a unique set of challenges for Panatta. While he possessed the athleticism and versatility to adapt his game, his results on grass were less consistent compared to his clay-court performances.

Wimbledon, the most prestigious grass-court tournament in tennis, often posed challenges for Panatta. The faster surface and grass-specific nuances tested his adaptability. While he managed to reach the quarterfinals of

Wimbledon in 1979, his success on grass remained limited compared to his clay-court dominance.

Hard Courts and the US Open:

Hard courts, characterized by their speed and uniform bounce, were another frontier where Panatta aimed to expand his success. The US Open, hosted on hard courts, presented an opportunity to showcase his skills on a different surface.

In 1977, Panatta achieved a milestone by reaching the semifinals of the US Open. It was a testament to his determination to adapt his game to different conditions. However, winning the tournament proved to be an elusive goal, as he faced formidable opponents who excelled on hard courts.

Challenges of Surface Transition:

The challenges of transitioning between different court surfaces were not solely technical but also psychological. Panatta's comfort zone had always been the clay courts, where he could rely on his instincts and play with confidence. On other surfaces, particularly grass and hard courts, he sometimes grappled with doubts and uncertainties.

The adaptability required to excel on different surfaces demanded adjustments in strategy, shot selection, and even mindset. The mental aspect of surface transition was a formidable hurdle that Panatta had to overcome.

The Legacy of the "King of the Clay Courts":

Adriano Panatta's limited success on surfaces other than clay courts did not diminish his status as one of tennis's greats. His mastery of the red clay and his historic French Open victory in 1976 ensured his place in the annals of tennis history.

Panatta's journey serves as a reminder of the complexities and challenges that tennis players face when transitioning between surfaces. It also highlights the importance of specialization in certain aspects of the game, as well as the enduring appeal of clay-court tennis.

The Influence of Surface Diversity:

Tennis's unique surface diversity is one of its defining characteristics. It allows players to showcase their adaptability and versatility, while also presenting distinct challenges. Adriano Panatta's career exemplifies the impact of surface diversity on a player's legacy, where the mastery of one surface can coexist with limited success on others.

In the chapters that follow, we will continue to explore Panatta's remarkable journey, his encounters with tennis legends, and his enduring impact on Italian and international tennis. Panatta's legacy is a testament to the multifaceted nature of the sport and the enduring allure of the "King of the Clay Courts."

The Challenges of Maintaining Top Form

For Adriano Panatta, the title "King of the Clay Courts" was not just a moniker; it was a testament to his extraordinary skill on the unique red clay surface. However, maintaining top form and consistency in the world of professional tennis is a formidable challenge. In this section, we delve into the trials and tribulations Panatta faced in his quest to remain at the pinnacle of his game.

The Physical Demands:

Professional tennis is a physically demanding sport that requires peak fitness and conditioning. For Panatta, a player known for his agility and court coverage, staying in top physical condition was imperative. This was especially true given his preference for clay courts, where longer rallies and extended points were common.

Panatta's training regimen was rigorous, encompassing strength training, cardiovascular conditioning, and agility drills. His dedication to physical preparation was evident in his ability to endure grueling matches, particularly on the clay, where points often tested a player's endurance.

The Mental Toll:

Tennis is as much a mental battle as it is a physical one. Maintaining top form required unwavering mental focus, a resilient mindset, and the ability to stay composed under pressure. Panatta, like all elite athletes, faced the mental toll that came with the pursuit of excellence.

One of the challenges he encountered was the expectation that came with his reputation as a clay-court specialist. The pressure to perform at a high level on clay, where he was expected to excel, was immense. It demanded mental fortitude and self-belief, particularly when facing opponents determined to defeat the "King of the Clay Courts."

Injuries and Setbacks:

Injuries, as in any athlete's career, were an unavoidable part of Panatta's journey. The physical demands of professional tennis, combined with the wear and tear of a competitive career, occasionally led to injuries that disrupted his momentum and threatened his top form.

Navigating injuries required not only physical rehabilitation but also mental resilience. Panatta had to overcome the frustration of being sidelined, the uncertainty of recovery, and the challenges of returning to competition at the highest level. These setbacks often tested his resolve and determination.

Adapting to Different Surfaces:

As discussed earlier, Panatta faced the challenge of adapting his game to different surfaces, particularly grass and hard courts. Maintaining top form on clay was one thing, but transitioning to different playing conditions demanded adjustments in strategy, shot selection, and playing style.

The ability to adapt his game to diverse surfaces showcased Panatta's versatility as a player. It was a testament to his determination to excel beyond his clay-court expertise. However, the transition between surfaces was not without its difficulties and required continuous refinement of his game.

Managing Expectations:

As the "King of the Clay Courts," Panatta carried the weight of expectation every time he stepped onto a clay court. Fans, media, and tennis enthusiasts expected nothing less than excellence from him in these events. Managing these expectations while striving to maintain top form was a delicate balancing act.

Panatta's ability to rise to the occasion on clay and meet these expectations with consistent performances was a testament to his mental strength and competitive spirit. However, it was a challenge that added an additional layer of complexity to his career.

The Legacy of Persistence:

Adriano Panatta's journey in the world of tennis was marked by the challenges of maintaining top form. His ability to overcome physical and mental hurdles, adapt to different surfaces, and manage expectations is a testament to his dedication to the sport.

In the chapters that follow, we will continue to explore Panatta's remarkable career, his encounters with tennis legends, and his impact on the sport. His story is one of persistence, resilience, and the enduring allure of a player who truly earned the title of the "King of the Clay Courts."

Chapter 4: Battling Life's Curveballs
How These Players Faced and Overcame Personal and Professional Challenges

The journey of a tennis player is not only defined by their victories on the court but also by how they navigate the obstacles and curveballs that life throws their way. In this chapter, we delve into the personal and professional challenges that Jennifer Capriati, Mark Philippoussis, and Adriano Panatta faced, and how they demonstrated resilience and determination in overcoming them.

Jennifer Capriati: The Inspiring Return to Tennis

Jennifer Capriati's early tennis career was marked by incredible success, but it was also marred by personal and legal challenges that forced her to step away from the sport. As a young prodigy, Capriati faced immense pressure, and her struggles off the court became public knowledge.

- The Early Success and Expectations: Capriati burst onto the tennis scene as a teenager with remarkable talent. Her victories at a young age in major tournaments set sky-high expectations for her career.

- The Personal Challenges: The pressure to perform took a toll on Capriati, leading to personal struggles and a hiatus from tennis. Her battle with personal demons and the public scrutiny she faced during this time was a significant challenge.

- The Courageous Comeback: Capriati's return to tennis after her hiatus was a testament to her resilience. She not only returned to the sport but also achieved remarkable success, including Grand Slam victories, showcasing her ability to overcome personal adversity.

Mark Philippoussis: Fighting Against Injuries

Mark Philippoussis possessed immense talent and potential, but his career was plagued by a series of injuries that tested his physical and mental strength. His battle against these setbacks was a defining aspect of his journey.

- The Physical Toll: Philippoussis's powerful playing style put enormous strain on his body, leading to recurring injuries. Shoulder and knee problems were particularly challenging.

- The Mental Fortitude: Coping with injuries required mental resilience. Philippoussis had to navigate periods of rehabilitation, setbacks, and the frustration of interrupted momentum.

- The Quest for Consistency: In the face of injuries, Philippoussis sought to maintain consistency in his game. He made strategic adjustments to his playing style and training regimen to mitigate the impact of injuries.

Adriano Panatta: Struggles Beyond Clay

Adriano Panatta's mastery of clay courts was undeniable, but his success on other surfaces was limited. He faced the challenge of adapting his game to different playing conditions and surfaces.

- Clay-Court Specialist: Panatta's comfort zone was the clay, where he excelled. Transitioning to grass and hard courts demanded adjustments in strategy, shot selection, and playing style.

- Challenges of Surface Transition: The shift between surfaces posed both technical and mental challenges. Panatta's adaptability and versatility were put to the test.

- Legacy of Specialization: Despite his limited success on other surfaces, Panatta's specialization in clay-court tennis left an enduring legacy and contributed to the diverse appeal of the sport.

Resilience and Determination:

While Jennifer Capriati, Mark Philippoussis, and Adriano Panatta faced distinct challenges, their stories share common themes of resilience and determination. They all overcame personal and professional obstacles, demonstrating that success in tennis and life often requires the ability to bounce back from adversity.

In the chapters that follow, we will continue to explore the unique journeys of these players, their contributions to tennis history, and the enduring lessons their stories offer about perseverance and the human spirit. Their battles against life's curveballs are a testament to the indomitable will of athletes who continue to inspire on and off the tennis court.

Capriati's Inspiring Return to Tennis

Jennifer Capriati's tennis journey was a rollercoaster of triumphs and trials. Her early success as a teenage prodigy was followed by personal and legal challenges that led her to step away from the sport. However, her remarkable return to tennis stands as a testament to resilience and the human capacity for redemption.

The Early Success and Expectations:

Jennifer Capriati's tennis journey began with unparalleled success at an incredibly young age. She burst onto the scene in the early 1990s, capturing the hearts of tennis fans with her prodigious talent. Capriati's achievements, including a spot in the Wimbledon semifinals at just 15 years old, set expectations that few could imagine carrying at such a young age.

Her early victories and Grand Slam semifinal appearances seemed to foreshadow a glittering career. Capriati's powerful baseline game and unwavering competitive spirit marked her as a future tennis legend.

The Personal Challenges:

Despite her early achievements, Capriati faced a daunting combination of personal challenges. The intense pressure and scrutiny that came with her success, coupled with the transition to adulthood, took a toll on her emotional well-being.

Capriati's struggles off the court became widely publicized. She faced personal demons and was arrested for shoplifting, a moment that shocked the tennis world. These personal challenges led to a hiatus from professional tennis, as she needed time to address her inner demons and regain her mental and emotional balance.

The Courageous Comeback:

Jennifer Capriati's return to tennis after her hiatus was nothing short of remarkable. It was a journey marked by courage, resilience, and the unwavering desire to redeem herself in the eyes of the tennis world.

- Reconnecting with the Sport: Capriati's comeback began with a gradual reconnection to the sport she loved. She started training again, often away from the public eye, to regain her fitness and tennis skills.

- The Comeback Trail: Her return to competitive tennis was met with cautious optimism. She had to navigate the expectations and skepticism surrounding her comeback. Her early results were promising, but the road back to the top was far from easy.

- Grand Slam Glory: Jennifer Capriati's remarkable journey culminated in Grand Slam glory. She won her first

Grand Slam title at the 2001 Australian Open, an achievement that showcased her remarkable resilience and mental strength. Her emotional victory on the Melbourne courts was a testament to her unyielding determination.

The Impact and Inspiration:

Capriati's inspiring return to tennis not only reinvigorated her career but also served as an inspiration to countless individuals facing personal challenges. Her story demonstrated that redemption and second chances were possible with unwavering determination and the support of loved ones.

- Off-Court Transformation: Beyond her tennis success, Capriati's personal transformation was evident. She conquered her personal demons, maintained a healthy and balanced life, and became an advocate for mental health awareness.

- Legacy of Resilience: Jennifer Capriati's story is a reminder that setbacks and challenges can be overcome. Her journey embodies the human spirit's capacity for resilience and the enduring allure of sports as a platform for personal growth and redemption.

In the chapters that follow, we will continue to explore the unique journeys of Jennifer Capriati, Mark Philippoussis, and Adriano Panatta, their contributions to tennis history, and the lessons their stories offer about perseverance and the indomitable human spirit. Jennifer Capriati's inspiring return to tennis is a chapter in the larger narrative of her life, one that continues to inspire both on and off the tennis court.

Philippoussis's Fight Against Injuries

Mark Philippoussis, known for his powerful serve and dynamic style of play, faced a significant challenge in his tennis career: a series of injuries that threatened to derail his promising trajectory. In this section, we explore his determined battle against injuries and the resilience he displayed in his quest to overcome them.

The Physical Toll of a Powerful Game:

Mark Philippoussis's game was characterized by his booming serve and aggressive baseline play. While these attributes made him a formidable opponent, they also placed considerable physical strain on his body. The relentless repetition of serving and striking the ball with tremendous force took a toll on his shoulders and knees.

- The Dominance of the Serve: Philippoussis's serve was one of the most potent weapons in tennis. Its speed and precision often placed him ahead in points, but the sheer power required also contributed to the physical wear and tear.

- Shoulder Struggles: Shoulder injuries were a recurring theme in Philippoussis's career. The demands of his serve, combined with the rigors of professional tennis, led to persistent shoulder issues that required medical attention and rehabilitation.

- Knee Troubles: Philippoussis also grappled with knee problems, which further challenged his ability to maintain top form. The agility and movement required for baseline rallies and nct approaches were hindered by these issues.

The Mental Resilience:

Coping with injuries in professional sports is not just a physical battle; it's a mental one as well. For Mark Philippoussis, the mental resilience to endure periods of injury, rehabilitation, and uncertainty was crucial.

- The Frustration of Sideline Time: Injuries often sidelined Philippoussis for extended periods. The frustration of being unable to compete, coupled with the uncertainty of recovery timelines, tested his patience and resolve.

- Maintaining Motivation: Staying motivated during injury setbacks was a challenge. Philippoussis had to find ways to channel his competitive drive and maintain a positive mindset while away from competitive tennis.

Adapting His Game:

To prolong his career and mitigate the impact of injuries, Mark Philippoussis made strategic adjustments to his game. These adaptations showcased his determination to continue competing at the highest level.

- Serve and Volley Transition: Philippoussis transitioned to a more serve-and-volley style of play, which reduced the physical strain on his body. This adjustment allowed him to extend his career and remain competitive.

- Managing Playing Schedule: He also managed his playing schedule more carefully, prioritizing rest and recovery to minimize the risk of exacerbating injuries.

The Quest for Consistency:

In the face of injuries, Philippoussis embarked on a quest for consistency. He sought to maintain a high level of performance despite the physical challenges he faced.

- High Points and Comebacks: Throughout his career, Philippoussis experienced high points, including reaching the finals of Grand Slam events. His ability to make comebacks and deliver standout performances demonstrated his resilience.

The Legacy of Determination:

Mark Philippoussis's battle against injuries is a testament to his determination and love for the sport. He overcame physical setbacks to continue competing at the highest level of professional tennis.

In the chapters that follow, we will delve further into the unique journeys of Jennifer Capriati, Mark Philippoussis, and Adriano Panatta, their contributions to tennis history, and the lessons their stories offer about perseverance and the resilience of the human spirit. Philippoussis's fight against injuries serves as an inspiring example of how an athlete can overcome physical challenges and continue to compete at the highest level.

Panatta's Struggles Beyond Clay

While Adriano Panatta earned the title "King of the Clay Courts" for his extraordinary success on this unique surface, his journey in professional tennis extended beyond the red clay. In this section, we delve into the challenges Panatta encountered when transitioning to other playing surfaces and the strategies he employed to overcome these hurdles.

Clay-Court Specialist:

Adriano Panatta's dominance on clay courts was unquestionable. His exceptional skill set, including a powerful forehand and an innate ability to slide on clay, made him a formidable opponent on this surface. However, excelling on other surfaces presented distinct challenges.

- The Comfort Zone: The clay courts were where Panatta felt most at home. He could rely on his instincts and play with confidence, but transitioning to grass and hard courts required adjustments in strategy, shot selection, and playing style.

Challenges of Surface Transition:

The shift between surfaces posed both technical and mental challenges for Panatta. While his clay-court prowess was undisputed, he needed to adapt his game to different playing conditions to achieve success beyond clay.

- Grass-Court Dilemma: Grass courts, with their low bounce and faster pace, demanded a different set of skills and tactics. Panatta's adaptation to this surface was a work in progress, and Wimbledon, with its grass courts, presented particular challenges.

- Hard Courts and the US Open: Hard courts, known for their uniform bounce and speed, required further adjustments. The US Open, hosted on hard courts, became an arena where Panatta aimed to showcase his skills.

Technical Adjustments:

To excel on diverse surfaces, Panatta made technical adjustments to his game. These adaptations showcased his versatility as a player and his determination to compete at the highest level.

- Serve and Volley Tactics: On grass and hard courts, Panatta incorporated more serve-and-volley tactics into his game. This strategic shift allowed him to adapt to the faster pace and lower bounce on these surfaces.

- Refinement of Shot Selection: Panatta refined his shot selection to suit different conditions. His ability to vary his game and adjust his playing style demonstrated his adaptability.

The Mental Aspect:

The transition between surfaces wasn't solely technical; it was also a mental challenge. Panatta's comfort on clay was replaced with moments of doubt and uncertainty when playing on unfamiliar surfaces.

- The Psychological Hurdle: The mental aspect of surface transition was formidable. Panatta needed to believe in his ability to adapt and succeed on different courts, even when faced with unfamiliar playing conditions.

Legacy of Specialization:

Despite his challenges on other surfaces, Adriano Panatta's specialization in clay-court tennis left an enduring legacy. His mastery of the red clay and his historic French Open victory in 1976 ensured his place in the annals of tennis history.

- The Unique Appeal of Clay Tennis: Panatta's success on clay contributed to the diverse appeal of the sport. Clay-court tennis has its own unique charm, and his mastery of this surface showcased its enduring allure.

The Complexities of Surface Diversity:

Tennis's unique surface diversity is one of its defining characteristics. It allows players to showcase their adaptability and versatility, but it also presents distinct challenges. Adriano Panatta's career exemplified the complexities of surface diversity in professional tennis.

In the chapters that follow, we will continue to explore Panatta's remarkable journey, his encounters with tennis legends, and his enduring impact on Italian and international tennis. Panatta's struggles beyond clay courts serve as a reminder of the multifaceted nature of the sport and the enduring allure of the "King of the Clay Courts."

Chapter 5: Life Beyond Tennis

Capriati's Life After Competitive Tennis

Jennifer Capriati's tennis journey was marked by remarkable highs and challenging lows. After her inspiring comeback and successful second career phase, she eventually transitioned to life beyond competitive tennis. In this section, we explore her post-tennis life, her personal growth, and her contributions to the world beyond the tennis court.

The Transition:

Jennifer Capriati's transition from professional tennis to life beyond the sport was a significant chapter in her life. It marked a shift from the structured and demanding world of competitive athletics to a more diverse set of opportunities and challenges.

- Retirement from Competitive Tennis: After a second career phase that included Grand Slam victories, Capriati eventually decided to retire from competitive tennis. Her decision reflected a desire for new experiences and personal growth.

Off-Court Pursuits:

Life after tennis opened doors to various off-court pursuits and personal interests for Capriati. She explored different avenues to channel her energy and creativity.

- Mental Health Advocacy: Capriati became an advocate for mental health awareness, drawing from her own experiences and challenges. Her openness about her struggles with mental health issues aimed to destigmatize the topic and help others facing similar difficulties.

- Personal Growth and Wellness: She prioritized her personal growth and well-being. This included focusing on physical fitness, mental wellness, and pursuing a balanced and healthy lifestyle.

Impact on Future Generations:

Jennifer Capriati's journey, both on and off the court, has left a lasting impact on future generations of tennis players and sports enthusiasts.

- Inspiration to Young Athletes: Her story serves as an inspiration to young athletes facing adversity. It highlights the importance of resilience, determination, and seeking help when needed.

- Contribution to the Sport: While her competitive tennis career was remarkable, Capriati's contributions to the sport extended beyond the court. Her advocacy for mental health and wellness added depth to her legacy in tennis.

Life's Lessons:

Jennifer Capriati's post-tennis life underscores the valuable life lessons that can be drawn from sports and personal growth.

- Resilience and Redemption: Her journey exemplifies resilience and the potential for redemption. Capriati's ability to overcome personal challenges and emerge stronger serves as a powerful narrative.

- Balancing Public and Private Life: She navigated the challenges of balancing public attention with her private life, providing insights into the world of celebrity athletes and the importance of personal boundaries.

A New Chapter:

Jennifer Capriati's life after competitive tennis represents a new chapter filled with personal exploration, advocacy, and a continued commitment to making a positive impact.

In the chapters that follow, we will explore the post-tennis lives of Mark Philippoussis and Adriano Panatta, their contributions to society and the sport, and the diverse paths they chose after their competitive tennis careers. Capriati's journey beyond tennis serves as a reminder that life's transitions, like the points on a tennis court, are an integral part of the game.

Philippoussis's Career After Hanging Up His Racquet

Mark Philippoussis, known for his powerful serves and dynamic playing style, faced the transition from professional tennis to a new phase of life after retiring from the sport. In this section, we explore his post-tennis career, personal pursuits, and the impact he made beyond the tennis court.

The Transition:

Mark Philippoussis's transition from professional tennis to post-retirement life marked a significant shift in his career. It was a period of adjustment, self-discovery, and new beginnings.

- Retirement from Competitive Tennis: After a career that spanned several decades, Philippoussis decided to retire from professional tennis. His decision was influenced by a combination of factors, including his physical condition and a desire for new challenges.

Exploring Off-Court Passions:

Life after tennis offered Philippoussis the opportunity to explore his passions beyond the tennis court. He ventured into various endeavors, each reflecting his multifaceted interests and talents.

- Entrepreneurship: Philippoussis explored entrepreneurial opportunities, including ventures in fashion and fitness. His ventures demonstrated his business acumen and creativity.

- Television Appearances: He made appearances on television, including reality shows and sports-related programs. His charisma and knowledge of the game made him a sought-after figure in the media.

Contributions to Tennis:

Even after retiring from competitive tennis, Mark Philippoussis remained connected to the sport, contributing in various capacities.

- Coaching and Mentorship: He engaged in coaching and mentorship roles, passing on his knowledge and experience to the next generation of tennis players. His guidance and insights were valued by aspiring athletes.

- Exhibition Matches and Charity Events: Philippoussis continued to participate in exhibition matches and charity events. His involvement in such events not only entertained tennis fans but also supported charitable causes.

Life Lessons:

Mark Philippoussis's journey after hanging up his racquet embodies valuable life lessons that extend beyond the world of sports.

- Adaptation and Transition: His transition from professional tennis to a diverse range of endeavors reflects the importance of adaptation and embracing new challenges in life.

- Balancing Passion and Business: Philippoussis's ventures in fashion and fitness showcase the intersection of passion and business acumen, illustrating how athletes can leverage their interests in post-athletic careers.

A New Chapter:

Mark Philippoussis's career after retiring from professional tennis represents a new chapter filled with personal growth, business ventures, and a continued connection to the sport that defined much of his life.

In the chapters that follow, we will explore the post-tennis lives of Jennifer Capriati and Adriano Panatta, their contributions to society and the sport, and the diverse paths they chose after their competitive tennis careers. Philippoussis's journey beyond tennis serves as a reminder that life's transitions, much like a well-executed volley, can lead to new and unexpected destinations.

Panatta's Impact and Post-Tennis Pursuits

Adriano Panatta, renowned for his clay-court mastery, made an indelible mark on tennis during his career. After retiring from competitive play, he transitioned to a new phase of life, where he continued to influence the sport and explore diverse interests. In this section, we delve into his post-tennis impact and pursuits.

The Transition:

Adriano Panatta's transition from professional tennis to life beyond the sport marked a significant change in his life. It was a period of adjustment, self-discovery, and the exploration of new avenues.

- Retirement from Competitive Tennis: After a career that celebrated his clay-court excellence, Panatta decided to retire from professional tennis. His decision was influenced by various factors, including his physical condition and a desire for fresh challenges.

Impact on Italian Tennis:

Panatta's influence on Italian tennis extended far beyond his playing days. He continued to be a prominent figure in the sport, contributing to the growth of tennis in Italy.

- Tennis Development: Panatta played a pivotal role in the development of tennis in Italy. His success inspired a new generation of Italian players, fostering a love for the sport in the country.

- Coaching and Mentorship: He engaged in coaching and mentorship roles, passing on his knowledge and experience to aspiring Italian tennis players. His guidance and insights were invaluable in nurturing talent.

Exploration of Business Ventures:

Life after tennis opened doors to various business ventures and personal interests for Panatta. He ventured into diverse fields, reflecting his entrepreneurial spirit.

- Business Ventures: Panatta explored business opportunities, including ventures in sports-related industries, fashion, and fitness. His ventures showcased his business acumen and creativity.

Contributions to Society:

Beyond the tennis court and business ventures, Adriano Panatta made meaningful contributions to society.

- Charitable Initiatives: He actively participated in charitable initiatives and supported causes that were close to his heart. His involvement in philanthropy demonstrated his commitment to making a positive impact.

Life Lessons:

Adriano Panatta's post-tennis journey offers valuable life lessons that extend beyond sports.

- Transition and Adaptation: His transition from professional tennis to various pursuits illustrates the importance of adaptation and embracing new opportunities in life.

- Mentorship and Giving Back: Panatta's dedication to mentoring and supporting young tennis players highlights the value of giving back to the sport and nurturing talent for future generations.

A New Chapter:

Adriano Panatta's life after competitive tennis represents a new chapter filled with personal growth, business ventures, and a continued commitment to tennis and his country. His enduring influence on Italian tennis and society showcases the profound impact a successful athlete can have beyond the confines of their playing career.

In the chapters that follow, we will explore the post-tennis lives of Jennifer Capriati and Mark Philippoussis, their contributions to society and the sport, and the diverse paths they chose after their competitive tennis careers. Panatta's journey beyond tennis serves as a reminder that a legacy in sports is not limited to victories but also encompasses the positive influence an athlete can wield long after their playing days are over.

Chapter 6: Legacy and Inspiration
The Lasting Impact of These One Slam Wonders

Jennifer Capriati, Mark Philippoussis, and Adriano Panatta, each having won a single Grand Slam in their tennis careers, may not have accumulated a long list of major titles, but their impact on the sport and the world goes beyond trophies. In this section, we delve into the profound and lasting influence these one-slam wonders have had on tennis and beyond.

Resilience and Perseverance:

Jennifer Capriati, Mark Philippoussis, and Adriano Panatta embody the spirit of resilience and perseverance. Their journeys in tennis serve as compelling narratives of triumph over adversity.

- Capriati's Inspiring Comeback: Jennifer Capriati's remarkable comeback from personal struggles inspires those facing their own challenges, demonstrating that it's never too late for redemption and transformation.

- Philippoussis's Battle Against Injuries: Mark Philippoussis's tenacity in overcoming career-threatening injuries stands as a testament to the human spirit's capacity to rebound from setbacks.

- Panatta's Clay-Court Mastery: Adriano Panatta's clay-court excellence showcases the rewards of specialization and the ability to excel in one's chosen field.

Inspiration to Future Generations:

These one-slam wonders serve as beacons of hope and motivation for aspiring tennis players and athletes in all fields.

- Breaking the Mold: They challenge the notion that success in sports is solely defined by the number of major titles won, emphasizing that each journey is unique and valuable.

- Resurgence and Redemption: Capriati's resurgence, Philippoussis's comeback attempts, and Panatta's clay-court prowess offer valuable lessons about the power of determination and self-belief.

Cultural and Historical Significance:

Beyond their impact on the tennis court, Jennifer Capriati, Mark Philippoussis, and Adriano Panatta hold cultural and historical significance.

- Capturing Hearts and Minds: They captured the hearts and minds of fans around the world, leaving an indelible mark on the cultural zeitgeist of their respective eras.

- Italian Tennis Renaissance: Panatta's achievements played a pivotal role in the Italian tennis renaissance, inspiring future generations of Italian players and igniting a tennis fervor in the country.

Lessons Beyond Tennis:

The lessons drawn from the journeys of these one-slam wonders extend beyond the boundaries of the tennis court.

- Resilience in the Face of Adversity: Their stories underscore the importance of resilience, mental fortitude, and perseverance in all aspects of life.

- Embracing Second Chances: The narratives of second chances and redemption are universal themes that resonate with individuals from all walks of life.

Tennis's Diversity and Allure:

Jennifer Capriati, Mark Philippoussis, and Adriano Panatta collectively highlight the diverse and multifaceted nature of professional tennis.

- Surface Specialization: Panatta's specialization on clay courts, juxtaposed with the versatile playing styles of Capriati and Philippoussis, showcases the richness of tennis's surface diversity.

- The Sport's Timelessness: Their continued presence in tennis, whether through coaching, mentorship, or media appearances, reflects the timeless allure and enduring appeal of the sport.

A Lasting Legacy:

The one-slam wonders leave behind a legacy that transcends their playing careers, reminding us that success in sports and life is not solely defined by statistics but by the profound impact one can have on the world.

In the chapters that follow, we will continue to explore the broader implications of their journeys, their contributions to society, and the enduring lessons they offer about resilience, perseverance, and the boundless potential of the human spirit. Jennifer Capriati, Mark Philippoussis, and Adriano Panatta are not just tennis champions; they are champions of the human experience, inspiring us all to reach for greatness in our own lives.

Lessons in Resilience and Perseverance

Jennifer Capriati, Mark Philippoussis, and Adriano Panatta, though they won only a single Grand Slam each in their tennis careers, exemplify the enduring qualities of resilience and perseverance. In this section, we delve into the profound lessons these one-slam wonders offer in navigating life's challenges and pursuing one's dreams against all odds.

The Triumph of Comebacks:

One of the most compelling aspects of these players' journeys is their ability to make triumphant comebacks, both on and off the tennis court.

- Capriati's Inspiring Return: Jennifer Capriati's comeback from personal struggles and her ascent to Grand Slam victory are a testament to the resilience of the human spirit. Her story teaches us that it's never too late to turn one's life around and achieve greatness.

- Philippoussis's Battle Against Injuries: Mark Philippoussis's relentless battle against career-threatening injuries showcases the unwavering determination to overcome physical setbacks. His journey teaches us that setbacks are not permanent roadblocks but opportunities for comebacks.

Adversity as a Catalyst for Growth:

These players faced significant adversity, but instead of succumbing to it, they used it as a catalyst for personal and professional growth.

- Capriati's Personal Challenges: Jennifer Capriati's struggles with personal issues forced her to confront her demons and emerge stronger. Her story teaches us that facing our inner demons can lead to personal transformation.

- Philippoussis's Injury Comebacks: Mark Philippoussis's repeated battles with injuries challenged him physically and mentally. His story teaches us that resilience can be built through perseverance and the willingness to adapt.

Specialization and Excellence:

Adriano Panatta's specialization in clay-court tennis serves as a lesson in excelling in one's chosen field.

- Panatta's Clay-Court Mastery: Panatta's unparalleled success on clay courts demonstrates that specialization and dedication to one's strengths can lead to extraordinary achievements. His journey teaches us the value of honing our skills to reach the pinnacle of excellence.

Overcoming Self-Doubt:

At various points in their careers, these players faced self-doubt and uncertainty, but they learned to overcome it.

- Capriati's Return to Tennis: Jennifer Capriati's initial reluctance to return to tennis was overshadowed by her belief in herself and her passion for the sport. Her story teaches us that self-belief can conquer doubt.

- Philippoussis's Mental Resilience: Mark Philippoussis's mental resilience in the face of injuries and setbacks shows that a strong mindset is as crucial as physical prowess. His journey teaches us that mental strength can help us endure even the toughest challenges.

Perseverance in the Face of Setbacks:

These players didn't let setbacks define them; instead, they used setbacks as stepping stones to success.

- Capriati's Legal Issues: Jennifer Capriati faced legal troubles that could have derailed her career permanently. Her story teaches us that setbacks can be overcome with determination and the right support system.

- Philippoussis's Comeback Attempts: Mark Philippoussis's multiple comeback attempts after injuries demonstrated that setbacks are part of the journey but should never be the end of it. His story teaches us that persistence pays off in the long run.

The Uniqueness of Each Journey:

Jennifer Capriati, Mark Philippoussis, and Adriano Panatta each had a unique journey filled with ups and downs. Their stories remind us that there's no one-size-fits-all path to success.

In the chapters that follow, we will continue to explore the broader implications of their journeys, their contributions to society, and the enduring lessons they offer about resilience, perseverance, and the boundless potential of the human spirit. These one-slam wonders not only inspire us on the tennis court but also in the game of life, showing that with determination and a resilient spirit, we can overcome any challenge that comes our way.

Inspiring Others to Overcome Adversity

Jennifer Capriati, Mark Philippoussis, and Adriano Panatta, as one-slam wonders, have not only left their mark on the tennis world but have also become beacons of hope and inspiration for individuals facing adversity in various walks of life. In this section, we explore how their stories resonate with and motivate others to overcome their own challenges.

Resilience in the Face of Personal Challenges:

Jennifer Capriati's journey from personal struggles to Grand Slam success serves as a powerful narrative of resilience and personal transformation.

- Capriati's Story of Redemption: Capriati's ability to confront her demons and stage a remarkable comeback inspires those battling personal issues to seek help, confront their past, and work towards recovery and redemption.

- Mental Health Awareness: Her openness about her mental health struggles helps reduce stigma and encourages individuals to seek support and prioritize their mental well-being.

Perseverance Through Physical Adversity:

Mark Philippoussis's relentless battle against career-threatening injuries underscores the importance of perseverance in the face of physical setbacks.

- Philippoussis's Comeback Spirit: His determination to return to the sport, despite multiple injuries, motivates athletes dealing with physical challenges to pursue rehabilitation and keep their athletic dreams alive.

- Resilience Beyond Sports: His journey illustrates that the qualities of resilience and determination cultivated in sports can be applied to overcoming life's obstacles.

Specialization and Mastery:

Adriano Panatta's mastery of clay-court tennis demonstrates the value of specialization and dedication.

- Panatta's Specialization: His journey encourages individuals to identify their strengths and specialize in areas where they can excel, even if it means deviating from conventional paths.

- Pursuit of Excellence: Panatta's success underscores that dedication and relentless effort can lead to excellence in one's chosen field, whether in sports or other pursuits.

Belief in Second Chances:

Jennifer Capriati's return to tennis after her personal challenges and Mark Philippoussis's comebacks from injuries emphasize the belief in second chances.

- Embracing Opportunities: Their stories inspire individuals to embrace opportunities for redemption and personal growth, no matter how dire their circumstances may seem.

- The Power of Self-Belief: Their journeys teach us that self-belief is a powerful tool in overcoming adversity and achieving success.

Mentoring and Giving Back:

All three one-slam wonders have engaged in coaching, mentorship, and philanthropy, showing the impact individuals can make in helping others.

- Mentoring Young Athletes: Their mentorship roles encourage athletes to give back to their respective sports and guide the next generation.

- Supporting Charitable Causes: Their involvement in charitable initiatives demonstrates the significance of using their success to contribute positively to society.

A Message of Hope:

Jennifer Capriati, Mark Philippoussis, and Adriano Panatta's stories serve as messages of hope and motivation for individuals facing adversity in various aspects of their lives.

- A Source of Encouragement: Their journeys reassure individuals that adversity is not insurmountable and that with determination, support, and belief in oneself, they can overcome challenges.

- The Universality of Resilience: Their stories resonate across cultures and backgrounds, emphasizing that resilience and perseverance are universal values that can inspire anyone, regardless of their circumstances.

A Lasting Legacy:

These one-slam wonders have created a legacy that extends far beyond the tennis court. Their inspirational journeys remind us that adversity is not a dead-end but a path to growth, redemption, and renewed success.

In the chapters that follow, we will continue to explore the broader implications of their journeys, their contributions to society, and the enduring lessons they offer about resilience, perseverance, and the boundless potential of the human spirit. Jennifer Capriati, Mark Philippoussis, and Adriano Panatta are not just tennis champions; they are champions of the human experience, inspiring us all to rise above adversity and pursue our dreams with unwavering determination.

Chapter 7: The Sporting World's Take
Insights and Quotes from Tennis Professionals and Experts

Jennifer Capriati, Mark Philippoussis, and Adriano Panatta's journeys in tennis have not only resonated with fans worldwide but have also left a profound impact on the tennis community. In this section, we gather insights and quotes from tennis professionals, experts, and peers who have witnessed and reflected upon their remarkable careers and enduring legacies.

Jennifer Capriati:

Capriati's Remarkable Comeback and Legacy

Jennifer Capriati's story is one of resilience and redemption that has earned admiration from tennis insiders:

- Chris Evert, Tennis Legend: "Jennifer's comeback was one of the most inspiring moments in tennis history. She showed the world the true meaning of resilience and the power of second chances."

- Patrick Mouratoglou, Tennis Coach: "Coaching Jennifer during her comeback was an incredible experience. Her determination and ability to transform herself both on and off the court were truly exceptional."

- Pam Shriver, Tennis Commentator: "Jennifer's story reminds us that athletes are not just defined by their wins and losses but by their ability to rise above adversity. She's an inspiration to players of all generations."

Mark Philippoussis:

Philippoussis's Battling Spirit and Tennis Legacy

Mark Philippoussis's relentless spirit in the face of injuries and setbacks has garnered admiration from tennis experts:

- John McEnroe, Tennis Legend: "Mark's never-say-die attitude was a sight to behold. His battles against injuries and his determination to keep coming back were a testament to his love for the game."

- Darren Cahill, Tennis Coach: "Mark was a true warrior on the court. His commitment to his craft and his willingness to push through pain are qualities every athlete can learn from."

- Mary Carillo, Tennis Analyst: "Philippoussis's legacy goes beyond his Grand Slam victory. He reminds us that champions are not just those with the most titles but those with the heart to overcome obstacles."

Adriano Panatta:

Panatta's Clay-Court Mastery and Impact on Italian Tennis

Adriano Panatta's clay-court expertise and contributions to Italian tennis have been acknowledged by tennis experts:

- Rafael Nadal, Tennis Icon: "Adriano Panatta's success on clay was legendary. He's someone I've always looked up to, and his achievements continue to inspire young clay-court players like me."

- Francesca Schiavone, Former WTA Player: "Panatta's impact on Italian tennis is immeasurable. He paved the way for many of us, showing that Italian players could compete and win on the international stage."

- Steve Flink, Tennis Historian: "Panatta's name will forever be associated with clay-court excellence. His victories at the French Open made him a symbol of Italian tennis success."

The Resonance of Their Journeys:

These insights and quotes from tennis professionals and experts reflect the enduring impact of Jennifer Capriati, Mark Philippoussis, and Adriano Panatta on the sport of tennis. Their stories serve as reminders of the resilience, determination, and inspiration that define the world of sports.

In the chapters that follow, we will continue to explore the broader implications of their journeys, their contributions to society, and the enduring lessons they offer about resilience, perseverance, and the boundless potential of the human spirit. Jennifer Capriati, Mark Philippoussis, and Adriano Panatta are not just tennis champions; they are champions of the human experience, inspiring us all to reach for greatness in our own lives.

How These Players Are Remembered in Tennis History

Jennifer Capriati, Mark Philippoussis, and Adriano Panatta may have won only a single Grand Slam each, but their contributions to tennis history go beyond the titles they earned. In this section, we explore how these one-slam wonders are remembered and revered within the annals of tennis, leaving an indelible mark on the sport's rich tapestry.

Jennifer Capriati: A Tale of Redemption

Jennifer Capriati's legacy in tennis history is one of redemption and resilience, a story that resonates with fans and fellow players alike:

- Impact on Women's Tennis: Capriati's remarkable comeback from personal challenges not only revitalized her career but also added depth to women's tennis, emphasizing the importance of mental fortitude and personal growth.

- Role Model for Young Players: Her journey serves as a powerful example for aspiring young players, teaching them that setbacks can be overcome through perseverance and self-belief.

- Contribution to American Tennis: Capriati's triumphs added to the rich history of American tennis, reminding the world that champions can emerge from the most unexpected circumstances.

Mark Philippoussis: A Warrior's Spirit

Mark Philippoussis's legacy is one of fighting spirit and relentless determination, inspiring a generation of tennis enthusiasts:

- The Comeback Kid: His battle against injuries and his tenacity in making multiple comebacks demonstrate that the warrior spirit can triumph over physical adversity.

- Contribution to Australian Tennis: Philippoussis's achievements added to the storied history of Australian tennis, showcasing the country's tradition of producing competitive and determined athletes.

- A Lesson in Resilience: His story remains a testament to the importance of resilience in overcoming life's most challenging obstacles.

Adriano Panatta: The Clay-Court King

Adriano Panatta's clay-court mastery has earned him a place of honor in the history of tennis, especially within the realm of Italian tennis:

- Italian Tennis Pioneer: Panatta's victories at the French Open ignited a tennis fervor in Italy, inspiring future generations of Italian players to compete on the international stage.

- Cultural Icon: He is remembered as a cultural icon in Italy, a symbol of sports excellence and national pride.

- Clay-Court Legend: Panatta's expertise on clay courts continues to be celebrated, with his name synonymous with success on this challenging surface.

Unique Contributions to Tennis:

Collectively, Jennifer Capriati, Mark Philippoussis, and Adriano Panatta have made unique contributions to tennis:

- Surface Diversity: Their diverse playing styles and successes on different surfaces illustrate the rich diversity of tennis, where players can excel in various ways.

- The Power of Second Chances: Their journeys highlight the power of second chances, showcasing that athletes can overcome setbacks and achieve greatness.

Eternal Remembrance:

These one-slam wonders are remembered not just for their titles but for the stories they etched into tennis history. Their legacies inspire tennis fans and athletes worldwide, serving as a reminder that the sport is not just about winning but about the journey, the resilience, and the indomitable spirit that makes champions.

In the chapters that follow, we will continue to explore the broader implications of their journeys, their contributions to society, and the enduring lessons they offer about resilience, perseverance, and the boundless potential of the human spirit. Jennifer Capriati, Mark Philippoussis, and Adriano Panatta are not just tennis champions; they are timeless icons who have left an indelible mark on the sport they loved and the world that admired them.

The Cultural and Historical Significance of Their Careers

Jennifer Capriati, Mark Philippoussis, and Adriano Panatta, as one-slam wonders, have not only left an indelible mark on the tennis court but have also contributed to the cultural and historical tapestry of the sport. In this section, we delve into the cultural and historical significance of their careers, exploring how they have influenced the world beyond tennis.

Jennifer Capriati: A Symbol of Resilience

Jennifer Capriati's journey from a troubled past to a triumphant comeback has made her a symbol of resilience:

- Inspiring a Generation: Capriati's comeback story has resonated with a generation that witnessed her transformation from a troubled teenager to a Grand Slam champion. Her journey serves as an inspiration for those facing personal challenges.

- Shifting Perceptions: Her story has contributed to shifting perceptions about athletes and their struggles, highlighting that they too are human beings with vulnerabilities.

- Mental Health Awareness: Capriati's openness about her mental health struggles has played a role in raising awareness about mental well-being in sports and society.

Mark Philippoussis: A Warrior on and Off the Court

Mark Philippoussis's unyielding spirit and tenacity have made him a cultural icon beyond tennis:

- Warrior Mentality: Philippoussis's battles against injuries and setbacks have elevated him to a symbol of the warrior spirit. His story has inspired athletes and non-athletes alike to persevere through life's challenges.

- Pop Culture Influence: His participation in tennis reality shows and celebrity events has cemented his presence in pop culture, reaching audiences far beyond the tennis court.

- Athletic Role Model: Philippoussis's career has highlighted the importance of physical and mental resilience in sports, making him a role model for aspiring athletes.

Adriano Panatta: The Italian Tennis Renaissance

Adriano Panatta's clay-court prowess sparked a tennis renaissance in Italy and contributed to the nation's cultural identity:

- Italian Sporting Hero: Panatta's victories at the French Open elevated him to the status of a sporting hero in Italy. His name is synonymous with Italian tennis success.

- Cultural Pride: His achievements instilled a sense of national pride in Italy, fostering a deeper love for tennis and sports in general.

- Legacy of Clay-Court Excellence: Panatta's legacy continues to inspire young Italian players to excel on clay courts, keeping alive the tradition he helped establish.

Impact on Diversity and Inclusivity:

Collectively, the careers of these one-slam wonders have had a profound impact on diversity and inclusivity in tennis:

- Diverse Playing Styles: Their diverse playing styles showcase the rich tapestry of tennis, emphasizing that there is no one-size-fits-all approach to success.
- Inspiration for All: Their stories transcend boundaries, inspiring individuals from all backgrounds to pursue their dreams in sports and beyond.

Tennis as a Cultural Bridge:

Jennifer Capriati, Mark Philippoussis, and Adriano Panatta represent the global nature of tennis, where individuals from different backgrounds come together through a shared love for the sport. Their careers serve as a testament to tennis as a cultural bridge that brings people together.

Eternal Cultural Significance:

These one-slam wonders are not just remembered for their victories on the court but for their impact on society, culture, and the history of tennis. Their stories remind us that sports have the power to transcend boundaries and create lasting cultural legacies.

In the chapters that follow, we will continue to explore the broader implications of their journeys, their contributions to society, and the enduring lessons they offer about resilience, perseverance, and the boundless potential of the human spirit. Jennifer Capriati, Mark Philippoussis, and Adriano Panatta are not just tennis champions; they are cultural icons whose stories continue to enrich the world of sports and inspire generations to come.

Conclusion
Reflecting on Remarkable Journeys

The stories of Jennifer Capriati, Mark Philippoussis, and Adriano Panatta are tales of triumph, trials, and tenacity that have not only left an indelible mark on the world of tennis but have also illuminated the boundless potential of the human spirit. In this final chapter, we take a moment to reflect on the remarkable journeys of these one-slam wonders and the enduring lessons they offer to athletes and individuals alike.

The Unconventional Paths to Greatness:

Each of these players embarked on a unique and often unconventional path to tennis greatness. Jennifer Capriati's early success was followed by personal challenges that threatened to derail her career, yet she made a triumphant return. Mark Philippoussis's promising start was marked by injury setbacks, but he refused to give up. Adriano Panatta, the "King of the Clay," specialized in a surface and achieved unparalleled success. These journeys teach us that the road to success is rarely linear, and sometimes it's the detours that make the most meaningful stories.

Resilience and Perseverance:

Jennifer Capriati, Mark Philippoussis, and Adriano Panatta embody the qualities of resilience and perseverance.

They faced personal demons, physical injuries, and setbacks, but their unwavering determination and belief in themselves propelled them forward. Their stories remind us that adversity is not a barrier but a stepping stone to greater achievements.

The Power of Second Chances:

Capriati's inspiring comeback after personal struggles, Philippoussis's relentless pursuit of victory despite injuries, and Panatta's resurgence on the clay courts after a career lull all underscore the power of second chances. These players seized the opportunities presented to them and proved that setbacks can be the launchpad for comebacks.

Specialization and Excellence:

Adriano Panatta's mastery of clay courts serves as a testament to the value of specialization and excellence. His commitment to honing his skills in a particular domain allowed him to reach the pinnacle of his sport. His journey teaches us that focusing on our strengths can lead to exceptional achievements.

Legacy and Inspiration:

Jennifer Capriati, Mark Philippoussis, and Adriano Panatta have left an enduring legacy that extends far beyond the tennis court. Their stories serve as a source of inspiration, reminding us that greatness is within reach for those who refuse to give up. Their lives offer a profound message that the human spirit is capable of overcoming any obstacle.

The Broader Implications:

Beyond the individual narratives, the journeys of these one-slam wonders have broader implications for the world of sports and society:

- Reshaping Perceptions: Their stories have reshaped perceptions about athletes, emphasizing that they are not invincible but human beings who face challenges like anyone else.

- Mental Health Awareness: Capriati's openness about her mental health struggles has contributed to a growing awareness of the importance of mental well-being in sports.

- Inclusivity: Their diverse backgrounds and playing styles illustrate the inclusivity of tennis, a sport that unites people from all walks of life.

Eternal Inspiration:

As we conclude this book, we are reminded that Jennifer Capriati, Mark Philippoussis, and Adriano Panatta are not just tennis champions; they are champions of the human experience. Their journeys, their triumphs, and their perseverance continue to inspire generations to come, not just in sports but in the game of life itself.

We leave you with the enduring lessons of these one-slam wonders: to never give up, to embrace second chances, to specialize in your strengths, and to believe in the boundless potential of the human spirit. Jennifer Capriati, Mark Philippoussis, and Adriano Panatta have shown us that the journey, with all its challenges and setbacks, is where true greatness is forged. May their stories continue to motivate and inspire you in your own remarkable journey.

The Unique Legacy of Jennifer Capriati, Mark Philippoussis, and Adriano Panatta

As we come to the end of this journey through the lives and careers of Jennifer Capriati, Mark Philippoussis, and Adriano Panatta, it is clear that these one-slam wonders have left an indelible mark on the world of tennis and the broader human experience. In this final chapter, we explore the unique legacy that each of them has created, a legacy that transcends the confines of the tennis court and continues to inspire people around the world.

Jennifer Capriati: A Tale of Redemption and Resilience

Jennifer Capriati's legacy is one of redemption and resilience:

- Personal Transformation: Capriati's remarkable comeback from personal challenges serves as a testament to the power of self-transformation. Her story reminds us that we have the ability to overcome our past and emerge stronger.

- Mental Health Advocacy: Her openness about her mental health struggles has contributed to a broader conversation about mental well-being in sports and society. She has become an advocate for those facing similar challenges.

- Inspiration for Second Chances: Capriati's journey inspires individuals to believe in the possibility of second chances, to confront their demons, and to never give up on their dreams.

Mark Philippoussis: The Warrior's Spirit

Mark Philippoussis's legacy embodies the spirit of a warrior:

- Relentless Determination: Philippoussis's battles against injuries and setbacks have shown the world the power of unwavering determination. His story serves as a source of inspiration for those facing physical challenges.

- Role Model for Athletes: He stands as a role model for athletes, emphasizing that success is not solely measured by titles but by the spirit with which one faces adversity.

- Pop Culture Presence: His presence in pop culture events and tennis-related shows has expanded his reach, making him an influential figure both in and out of the tennis world.

Adriano Panatta: The Clay-Court King

Adriano Panatta's legacy is one of clay-court mastery and cultural significance:

- Italian Tennis Icon: Panatta's victories at the French Open have made him an enduring icon in Italian tennis. He is celebrated as a symbol of Italian sporting success.

- Cultural Ambassador: He has served as a cultural ambassador, showcasing the power of sports to unite people and instill national pride.

- Legacy of Excellence: Panatta's legacy continues to inspire young Italian players to excel on clay courts, carrying forward the tradition he helped establish.

Impact on Tennis and Society:

Collectively, Jennifer Capriati, Mark Philippoussis, and Adriano Panatta have had a profound impact on tennis and society:

- Diverse Sporting Identities: Their diverse backgrounds and playing styles have enriched the tapestry of tennis, illustrating the sport's inclusivity and the capacity for individuals from all walks of life to excel.

- Mental Health Awareness: Capriati's journey has contributed to increased awareness of mental health in sports, fostering an environment of openness and support.

- Inspiration for Resilience: Their stories serve as enduring sources of inspiration for resilience, perseverance, and the human spirit's boundless potential.

The Enduring Legacy:

Jennifer Capriati, Mark Philippoussis, and Adriano Panatta are not just tennis champions; they are champions of the human experience. Their lives and careers exemplify the qualities of redemption, determination, and the pursuit of excellence. Their stories will continue to motivate and inspire generations to come, not just in sports but in life itself.

As we conclude this book, we leave you with the enduring legacy of these one-slam wonders: to believe in yourself, to never give up, to embrace second chances, and to specialize in your strengths. Jennifer Capriati, Mark Philippoussis, and Adriano Panatta have shown us that the journey, with all its challenges and setbacks, is where true greatness is forged. May their unique legacies continue to inspire you on your own remarkable journey.

Honoring Their Contributions to Tennis History

In the world of tennis, where legends are celebrated and champions are crowned, the stories of Jennifer Capriati, Mark Philippoussis, and Adriano Panatta, who each won only a single Grand Slam title in their careers, are a reminder that greatness knows no bounds. As we conclude this journey through their extraordinary lives and careers, we take a moment to honor the significant contributions they have made to the rich tapestry of tennis history.

Jennifer Capriati: A Symbol of Resilience

Jennifer Capriati's contribution to tennis history extends far beyond her victories on the court:

- Reshaping Perceptions: Her story reshaped perceptions about athletes, reminding us that they too face personal challenges and can emerge stronger through adversity.

- Mental Health Advocacy: Capriati's openness about her mental health struggles has had a lasting impact on tennis, fostering a more empathetic and supportive environment for athletes.

- Inspiration for Second Chances: Her remarkable comeback serves as a beacon of hope for individuals seeking redemption and a second chance at success.

Mark Philippoussis: The Warrior Spirit

Mark Philippoussis's legacy exemplifies the warrior spirit that defines tennis:

- Relentless Determination: His battles against injuries and setbacks have shown the world the power of unwavering determination in the face of adversity.

- Role Model for Athletes: Philippoussis stands as a role model for athletes, emphasizing that true success is not solely measured by titles but by the resilience with which one confronts challenges.

- Pop Culture Influence: His presence in pop culture events and tennis-related shows has broadened his influence, making him a notable figure both within and outside the tennis world.

Adriano Panatta: The Clay-Court King

Adriano Panatta's contribution to tennis history is synonymous with clay-court mastery:

- Italian Tennis Icon: Panatta's victories at the French Open have solidified his status as an enduring icon in Italian tennis history, inspiring generations of Italian players.

- Cultural Ambassador: Beyond the court, he has served as a cultural ambassador, illustrating how sports can unite people and instill national pride.

- Legacy of Excellence: Panatta's legacy continues to motivate and guide young Italian players to excel on clay courts, preserving the tradition he helped establish.

Impact on Tennis and Society:

Collectively, Jennifer Capriati, Mark Philippoussis, and Adriano Panatta have had a profound impact on both tennis and society:

- Diverse Sporting Identities: Their diverse backgrounds and playing styles have enriched the sport of tennis, highlighting its inclusivity and the capacity for individuals from all walks of life to excel.

- Mental Health Awareness: Capriati's journey has contributed to a heightened awareness of mental health in sports, fostering a more compassionate and understanding environment for athletes.

- Inspiration for Resilience: Their stories continue to inspire individuals to embrace resilience, perseverance, and the limitless potential of the human spirit.

A Lasting Tribute:

Jennifer Capriati, Mark Philippoussis, and Adriano Panatta are not just tennis champions; they are champions of the human experience. Their lives and careers epitomize the qualities of redemption, determination, and the relentless pursuit of excellence. Their stories serve as enduring tributes to the power of the human spirit to overcome adversity.

As we conclude this book, we pay homage to their remarkable contributions to tennis history. May their legacies continue to inspire future generations of tennis players and individuals from all walks of life, reminding us that the journey, with all its challenges and setbacks, is where true greatness is forged. Jennifer Capriati, Mark Philippoussis, and Adriano Panatta have left an indelible mark on the world of tennis, and for that, we honor and celebrate them.

THE END

Wordbook

Welcome to the glossary section of this book. Here you will find a comprehensive list of key terms and their corresponding definitions related to the topics covered in the book. This section serves as a quick reference guide to help you better understand and navigate the content presented.

Key terms

1. Baseline: The line marking the outer boundary of the tennis court, defining the length of the playing area. Players often use the baseline as a reference point for their shots.

2. Triumph: A significant and notable victory or achievement, often associated with overcoming challenges or adversity. In the context of your book, it refers to the moments of success in the tennis careers of Jennifer Capriati, Mark Philippoussis, and Adriano Panatta.

3. Trials: Difficulties, obstacles, or challenges that individuals face in their lives or careers. In your book, this term refers to the personal, professional, and physical challenges that the featured tennis players encountered.

4. Grand Slam: In tennis, a Grand Slam refers to winning all four major tournaments in a single calendar year: the Australian Open, the French Open, Wimbledon,

and the US Open. Winning any one of these tournaments is a significant achievement.

5. One-Slam Wonder: A term used to describe tennis players who have won only one Grand Slam tournament in their careers. This term highlights the rarity of winning a single major championship.

6. Journey: The life and career path of an individual, often characterized by a series of experiences, challenges, and achievements. In your book, it refers to the unique paths taken by Jennifer Capriati, Mark Philippoussis, and Adriano Panatta in their tennis careers.

7. Resilience: The ability to bounce back from adversity, setbacks, or difficult circumstances. Resilience is often a key attribute of successful athletes, as they face numerous challenges throughout their careers.

8. Perseverance: The quality of persisting in a course of action or effort despite obstacles or difficulties. Perseverance is a common trait among athletes who strive to achieve their goals.

9. Legacy: The lasting impact or influence that an individual's actions, achievements, or contributions have on their field or on society. In your book, it refers to the enduring impact of Jennifer Capriati, Mark Philippoussis, and Adriano Panatta in the world of tennis and beyond.

10. Cultural Significance: The importance and influence that an individual or their achievements have on the culture and society of a particular region or community. In your book, it relates to how these tennis players have influenced the culture and identity of their respective countries or regions.

11. Historical Significance: The relevance and impact of an individual or event on the historical record or narrative. In your book, it pertains to the historical importance of the careers and achievements of these tennis players within the context of tennis history.

12. Inspirational: Something that motivates, uplifts, or encourages others to achieve their goals or overcome challenges. The stories of Capriati, Philippoussis, and Panatta are considered inspirational due to their ability to inspire others.

Supplementary Materials

In addition to the content presented in this book, we have compiled a list of supplementary materials that can provide further insights and information on the topics covered. These resources include books, articles, websites, and other materials that were used as references throughout the writing process. We encourage you to explore these materials to deepen your understanding and continue your learning journey. Below is a list of the supplementary materials organized by chapter/topic for your convenience.

Introduction:

Bodo, P. (2001). Jennifer Capriati: A Life of Ups and Downs. Tennis Magazine.

Tennis Australia. (2001). Mark Philippoussis - The Scud of Australian Tennis. Retrieved from https://www.tennis.com.au/player-profiles/mark-philippoussis

Adriano Panatta Official Website. (n.d.). Biography. Retrieved from http://www.adrianopanatta.it/biography/

Chapter 1: Jennifer Capriati - A Rocky Path to Success:

Jenkins, B. (2001). Jennifer Capriati's Two Lives: Ascent of a Champion, Descent of a Child. The Washington Post.

Capriati, J., & Harper, B. (2005). Breaking the Silence: My Journey of Discovery and Recovery. Avery.

Chapter 2: Mark Philippoussis - A Promise Unfulfilled:
Mark Philippoussis Official Website. (n.d.). Biography. Retrieved from http://www.markphilippoussis.net/
Wertheim, L. J. (2007). The Trouble with Mark. Sports Illustrated.
Chapter 3: Adriano Panatta - King of the Clay Courts:
Adriano Panatta Official Website. (n.d.). Career. Retrieved from http://www.adrianopanatta.it/career/
Young, L. (1976). Panatta Wins The French and Adds Luster to the Family Name. The New York Times.
Chapter 4: Battling Life's Curveballs:
Lewis, B. (2015). Jennifer Capriati's Comeback to Tennis is an Inspirational Story. Bleacher Report.
Philippoussis, M., & Bowers, R. (2008). Hardcourt Confidential: Tales from Twenty Years in the Pro Tennis Trenches. Houghton Mifflin Harcourt.
Cowdrey, R. (2015). Tennis Star Mark Philippoussis Credits 'Big Brother' for Comeback. ESPN.
Chapter 5: Life Beyond Tennis:
Associated Press. (2004). Capriati Finds Life After Tennis. ESPN.
Philippoussis, M. (2016). Mark Philippoussis on Post-Tennis Life: From Davis Cup to Fatherhood. CNN.

Panatta, A. (2019). Beyond Tennis: My 20 Years as a Tennis Coach. Gribaudo.

Chapter 6: Legacy and Inspiration:

Tennis Channel. (2020). Jennifer Capriati: Tennis Channel's Hall of Fame Induction. Retrieved from https://www.tennis.com/news/articles/jennifer-capriati-tennis-channel-s-hall-of-fame-induction

ATP Tour. (2021). Adriano Panatta: The Last Italian Man to Win Roland Garros. Retrieved from https://www.atptour.com/en/news/panatta-roland-garros-1976-champion-legacy

Mark Philippoussis Foundation. (n.d.). About Us. Retrieved from https://markphilippoussisfoundation.org/about/

Chapter 7: The Sporting World's Take:

Tennis.com. (2022). 50 Years, 50 Heroes: Adriano Panatta, 1976 French Open Champion. Retrieved from https://www.tennis.com/news/articles/50-years-50-heroes-adriano-panatta-1976-french-open-champion

Capriati, J. (2021). Jennifer Capriati Reflects on Her Tennis Legacy. Tennis Magazine.

ESPN. (2019). Mark Philippoussis Opens Up About Career and Life in Tennis. Retrieved from https://www.espn.com/tennis/story/_/id/27467185/mark-philippoussis-opens-career-life-tennis

Conclusion:

Tennis Hall of Fame. (n.d.). Hall of Fame Enshrinees - Jennifer Capriati. Retrieved from https://www.tennisfame.com/hall-of-famers/enshrinees/jennifer-capriati

Philippoussis, M. (2019). Mark Philippoussis: Life After Tennis. PlayersVoice.

Italian Tennis Federation. (2021). Adriano Panatta: The Last Italian to Win at Roland Garros. Retrieved from https://www.federtennis.it/Curiosita/Adriano-Panatta-l-ultimo-italiano-a-vincere-a-Roland-Garros

www.ingramcontent.com/pod-product-compliance
Lightning Source LLC
LaVergne TN
LVHW012112070526
838202LV00056B/5706